C-2105   CAREER EXAMINATION SERIES

This is your
PASSBOOK for...

Station Supervisor

Test Preparation Study Guide
Questions & Answers

NATIONAL LEARNING CORPORATION®

COPYRIGHT NOTICE

This book is SOLELY intended for, is sold ONLY to, and its use is RESTRICTED to individual, bona fide applicants or candidates who qualify by virtue of having seriously filed applications for appropriate license, certificate, professional and/or promotional advancement, higher school matriculation, scholarship, or other legitimate requirements of education and/or governmental authorities.

This book is NOT intended for use, class instruction, tutoring, training, duplication, copying, reprinting, excerption, or adaptation, etc., by:

1) Other publishers
2) Proprietors and/or Instructors of "Coaching" and/or Preparatory Courses
3) Personnel and/or Training Divisions of commercial, industrial, and governmental organizations
4) Schools, colleges, or universities and/or their departments and staffs, including teachers and other personnel
5) Testing Agencies or Bureaus
6) Study groups which seek by the purchase of a single volume to copy and/or duplicate and/or adapt this material for use by the group as a whole without having purchased individual volumes for each of the members of the group
7) Et al.

Such persons would be in violation of appropriate Federal and State statutes.

PROVISION OF LICENSING AGREEMENTS – Recognized educational, commercial, industrial, and governmental institutions and organizations, and others legitimately engaged in educational pursuits, including training, testing, and measurement activities, may address request for a licensing agreement to the copyright owners, who will determine whether, and under what conditions, including fees and charges, the materials in this book may be used them. In other words, a licensing facility exists for the legitimate use of the material in this book on other than an individual basis. However, it is asseverated and affirmed here that the material in this book CANNOT be used without the receipt of the express permission of such a licensing agreement from the Publishers. Inquiries re licensing should be addressed to the company, attention rights and permissions department.

All rights reserved, including the right of reproduction in whole or in part, in any form or by any means, electronic or mechanical, including photocopying, recording, or by any information storage and retrieval system, without permission in writing from the Publisher.

Copyright © 2024 by
National Learning Corporation

212 Michael Drive, Syosset, NY 11791
(516) 921-8888 • www.passbooks.com
E-mail: info@passbooks.com

PUBLISHED IN THE UNITED STATES OF AMERICA

PASSBOOK® SERIES

THE *PASSBOOK® SERIES* has been created to prepare applicants and candidates for the ultimate academic battlefield – the examination room.

At some time in our lives, each and every one of us may be required to take an examination – for validation, matriculation, admission, qualification, registration, certification, or licensure.

Based on the assumption that every applicant or candidate has met the basic formal educational standards, has taken the required number of courses, and read the necessary texts, the *PASSBOOK® SERIES* furnishes the one special preparation which may assure passing with confidence, instead of failing with insecurity. Examination questions – together with answers – are furnished as the basic vehicle for study so that the mysteries of the examination and its compounding difficulties may be eliminated or diminished by a sure method.

This book is meant to help you pass your examination provided that you qualify and are serious in your objective.

The entire field is reviewed through the huge store of content information which is succinctly presented through a provocative and challenging approach – the question-and-answer method.

A climate of success is established by furnishing the correct answers at the end of each test.

You soon learn to recognize types of questions, forms of questions, and patterns of questioning. You may even begin to anticipate expected outcomes.

You perceive that many questions are repeated or adapted so that you can gain acute insights, which may enable you to score many sure points.

You learn how to confront new questions, or types of questions, and to attack them confidently and work out the correct answers.

You note objectives and emphases, and recognize pitfalls and dangers, so that you may make positive educational adjustments.

Moreover, you are kept fully informed in relation to new concepts, methods, practices, and directions in the field.

You discover that you are actually taking the examination all the time: you are preparing for the examination by "taking" an examination, not by reading extraneous and/or supererogatory textbooks.

In short, this PASSBOOK®, used directedly, should be an important factor in helping you to pass your test.

STATION SUPERVISOR

DUTIES
To be in responsible charge of a major subdivision of the Station Department. Station Supervisors, under general supervision, supervise staff engaged in the receipt and remittance of revenue, customer service, the operation of station controls, the manual, mechanical, and specialized cleaning of stations and environs, track tile cleaning, and refuse collection. The supervise and assign station personnel; conduct booth audits to ensure revenue accountability; provide customer service; conduct inspections and recommend appropriate action to improve the condition of stations and station equipment; prepare and analyze reports; drive a motor vehicle; and perform such other duties as the authority is authorized by law to prescribe in its regulations.

EXAMPLES OF TYPICAL TASKS
Is in charge of a major subdivision of the Station Department and the associated forces engaged in the receipt and collection of revenue, the station cleaning and the manning of station controls. Supervises and plans the assignment of station personnel. Makes inspection and takes appropriate action on condition of stations and station equipment. Prepares budgets. Evaluates equipment and materials. Plans and administers the revenue record system. Analyzes records and makes recommendations. Plans investigations and makes reports. Makes decision involving movement of passengers during emergencies.

SCOPE OF THE EXAMINATION
The written test may include questions designed to test for knowledge of the work procedures of subordinate employees in the Station Department and the ability to supervise them; ability to manage a major subdivision of the Station Department; ability to understand and interpret given rules and regulations and Department procedures; ability to conduct investigations; knowledge of job-related arithmetic; knowledge of the transit authority train system and its operations; proper use of materials and supplies; safe and efficient work procedures; and other related items.

HOW TO TAKE A TEST

I. YOU MUST PASS AN EXAMINATION

A. WHAT EVERY CANDIDATE SHOULD KNOW

Examination applicants often ask us for help in preparing for the written test. What can I study in advance? What kinds of questions will be asked? How will the test be given? How will the papers be graded?

As an applicant for a civil service examination, you may be wondering about some of these things. Our purpose here is to suggest effective methods of advance study and to describe civil service examinations.

Your chances for success on this examination can be increased if you know how to prepare. Those "pre-examination jitters" can be reduced if you know what to expect. You can even experience an adventure in good citizenship if you know why civil service exams are given.

B. WHY ARE CIVIL SERVICE EXAMINATIONS GIVEN?

Civil service examinations are important to you in two ways. As a citizen, you want public jobs filled by employees who know how to do their work. As a job seeker, you want a fair chance to compete for that job on an equal footing with other candidates. The best-known means of accomplishing this two-fold goal is the competitive examination.

Exams are widely publicized throughout the nation. They may be administered for jobs in federal, state, city, municipal, town or village governments or agencies.

Any citizen may apply, with some limitations, such as the age or residence of applicants. Your experience and education may be reviewed to see whether you meet the requirements for the particular examination. When these requirements exist, they are reasonable and applied consistently to all applicants. Thus, a competitive examination may cause you some uneasiness now, but it is your privilege and safeguard.

C. HOW ARE CIVIL SERVICE EXAMS DEVELOPED?

Examinations are carefully written by trained technicians who are specialists in the field known as "psychological measurement," in consultation with recognized authorities in the field of work that the test will cover. These experts recommend the subject matter areas or skills to be tested; only those knowledges or skills important to your success on the job are included. The most reliable books and source materials available are used as references. Together, the experts and technicians judge the difficulty level of the questions.

Test technicians know how to phrase questions so that the problem is clearly stated. Their ethics do not permit "trick" or "catch" questions. Questions may have been tried out on sample groups, or subjected to statistical analysis, to determine their usefulness.

Written tests are often used in combination with performance tests, ratings of training and experience, and oral interviews. All of these measures combine to form the best-known means of finding the right person for the right job.

II. HOW TO PASS THE WRITTEN TEST

A. NATURE OF THE EXAMINATION

To prepare intelligently for civil service examinations, you should know how they differ from school examinations you have taken. In school you were assigned certain definite pages to read or subjects to cover. The examination questions were quite detailed and usually emphasized memory. Civil service exams, on the other hand, try to discover your present ability to perform the duties of a position, plus your potentiality to learn these duties. In other words, a civil service exam attempts to predict how successful you will be. Questions cover such a broad area that they cannot be as minute and detailed as school exam questions.

In the public service similar kinds of work, or positions, are grouped together in one "class." This process is known as *position-classification*. All the positions in a class are paid according to the salary range for that class. One class title covers all of these positions, and they are all tested by the same examination.

B. FOUR BASIC STEPS

1) Study the announcement

How, then, can you know what subjects to study? Our best answer is: "Learn as much as possible about the class of positions for which you've applied." The exam will test the knowledge, skills and abilities needed to do the work.

Your most valuable source of information about the position you want is the official exam announcement. This announcement lists the training and experience qualifications. Check these standards and apply only if you come reasonably close to meeting them.

The brief description of the position in the examination announcement offers some clues to the subjects which will be tested. Think about the job itself. Review the duties in your mind. Can you perform them, or are there some in which you are rusty? Fill in the blank spots in your preparation.

Many jurisdictions preview the written test in the exam announcement by including a section called "Knowledge and Abilities Required," "Scope of the Examination," or some similar heading. Here you will find out specifically what fields will be tested.

2) Review your own background

Once you learn in general what the position is all about, and what you need to know to do the work, ask yourself which subjects you already know fairly well and which need improvement. You may wonder whether to concentrate on improving your strong areas or on building some background in your fields of weakness. When the announcement has specified "some knowledge" or "considerable knowledge," or has used adjectives like "beginning principles of..." or "advanced ... methods," you can get a clue as to the number and difficulty of questions to be asked in any given field. More questions, and hence broader coverage, would be included for those subjects which are more important in the work. Now weigh your strengths and weaknesses against the job requirements and prepare accordingly.

3) Determine the level of the position

Another way to tell how intensively you should prepare is to understand the level of the job for which you are applying. Is it the entering level? In other words, is this the position in which beginners in a field of work are hired? Or is it an intermediate or advanced level? Sometimes this is indicated by such words as "Junior" or "Senior" in the class title. Other jurisdictions use Roman numerals to designate the level – Clerk I, Clerk II, for example. The word "Supervisor" sometimes appears in the title. If the level is not indicated by the title, check the description of duties. Will you be working under very close supervision, or will you have responsibility for independent decisions in this work?

4) Choose appropriate study materials

Now that you know the subjects to be examined and the relative amount of each subject to be covered, you can choose suitable study materials. For beginning level jobs, or even advanced ones, if you have a pronounced weakness in some aspect of your training, read a modern, standard textbook in that field. Be sure it is up to date and has general coverage. Such books are normally available at your library, and the librarian will be glad to help you locate one. For entry-level positions, questions of appropriate difficulty are chosen – neither highly advanced questions, nor those too simple. Such questions require careful thought but not advanced training.

If the position for which you are applying is technical or advanced, you will read more advanced, specialized material. If you are already familiar with the basic principles of your field, elementary textbooks would waste your time. Concentrate on advanced textbooks and technical periodicals. Think through the concepts and review difficult problems in your field.

These are all general sources. You can get more ideas on your own initiative, following these leads. For example, training manuals and publications of the government agency which employs workers in your field can be useful, particularly for technical and professional positions. A letter or visit to the government department involved may result in more specific study suggestions, and certainly will provide you with a more definite idea of the exact nature of the position you are seeking.

III. KINDS OF TESTS

Tests are used for purposes other than measuring knowledge and ability to perform specified duties. For some positions, it is equally important to test ability to make adjustments to new situations or to profit from training. In others, basic mental abilities not dependent on information are essential. Questions which test these things may not appear as pertinent to the duties of the position as those which test for knowledge and information. Yet they are often highly important parts of a fair examination. For very general questions, it is almost impossible to help you direct your study efforts. What we can do is to point out some of the more common of these general abilities needed in public service positions and describe some typical questions.

1) General information

Broad, general information has been found useful for predicting job success in some kinds of work. This is tested in a variety of ways, from vocabulary lists to questions about current events. Basic background in some field of work, such as sociology or economics, may be sampled in a group of questions. Often these are principles which have become familiar to most persons through exposure rather than through formal training. It is difficult to advise you how to study for these questions; being alert to the world around you is our best suggestion.

2) Verbal ability

An example of an ability needed in many positions is verbal or language ability. Verbal ability is, in brief, the ability to use and understand words. Vocabulary and grammar tests are typical measures of this ability. Reading comprehension or paragraph interpretation questions are common in many kinds of civil service tests. You are given a paragraph of written material and asked to find its central meaning.

3) Numerical ability

Number skills can be tested by the familiar arithmetic problem, by checking paired lists of numbers to see which are alike and which are different, or by interpreting charts and graphs. In the latter test, a graph may be printed in the test booklet which you are asked to use as the basis for answering questions.

4) Observation

A popular test for law-enforcement positions is the observation test. A picture is shown to you for several minutes, then taken away. Questions about the picture test your ability to observe both details and larger elements.

5) Following directions

In many positions in the public service, the employee must be able to carry out written instructions dependably and accurately. You may be given a chart with several columns, each column listing a variety of information. The questions require you to carry out directions involving the information given in the chart.

6) Skills and aptitudes

Performance tests effectively measure some manual skills and aptitudes. When the skill is one in which you are trained, such as typing or shorthand, you can practice. These tests are often very much like those given in business school or high school courses. For many of the other skills and aptitudes, however, no short-time preparation can be made. Skills and abilities natural to you or that you have developed throughout your lifetime are being tested.

Many of the general questions just described provide all the data needed to answer the questions and ask you to use your reasoning ability to find the answers. Your best preparation for these tests, as well as for tests of facts and ideas, is to be at your physical and mental best. You, no doubt, have your own methods of getting into an exam-taking mood and keeping "in shape." The next section lists some ideas on this subject.

IV. KINDS OF QUESTIONS

Only rarely is the "essay" question, which you answer in narrative form, used in civil service tests. Civil service tests are usually of the short-answer type. Full instructions for answering these questions will be given to you at the examination. But in case this is your first experience with short-answer questions and separate answer sheets, here is what you need to know:

1) Multiple-choice Questions

Most popular of the short-answer questions is the "multiple choice" or "best answer" question. It can be used, for example, to test for factual knowledge, ability to solve problems or judgment in meeting situations found at work.

A multiple-choice question is normally one of three types—
- It can begin with an incomplete statement followed by several possible endings. You are to find the one ending which *best* completes the statement, although some of the others may not be entirely wrong.
- It can also be a complete statement in the form of a question which is answered by choosing one of the statements listed.

- It can be in the form of a problem – again you select the best answer.

Here is an example of a multiple-choice question with a discussion which should give you some clues as to the method for choosing the right answer:

When an employee has a complaint about his assignment, the action which will *best* help him overcome his difficulty is to
   A. discuss his difficulty with his coworkers
   B. take the problem to the head of the organization
   C. take the problem to the person who gave him the assignment
   D. say nothing to anyone about his complaint

In answering this question, you should study each of the choices to find which is best. Consider choice "A" – Certainly an employee may discuss his complaint with fellow employees, but no change or improvement can result, and the complaint remains unresolved. Choice "B" is a poor choice since the head of the organization probably does not know what assignment you have been given, and taking your problem to him is known as "going over the head" of the supervisor. The supervisor, or person who made the assignment, is the person who can clarify it or correct any injustice. Choice "C" is, therefore, correct. To say nothing, as in choice "D," is unwise. Supervisors have and interest in knowing the problems employees are facing, and the employee is seeking a solution to his problem.

2) True/False Questions

The "true/false" or "right/wrong" form of question is sometimes used. Here a complete statement is given. Your job is to decide whether the statement is right or wrong.

SAMPLE: A roaming cell-phone call to a nearby city costs less than a non-roaming call to a distant city.

This statement is wrong, or false, since roaming calls are more expensive.

This is not a complete list of all possible question forms, although most of the others are variations of these common types. You will always get complete directions for answering questions. Be sure you understand *how* to mark your answers – ask questions until you do.

V. RECORDING YOUR ANSWERS

Computer terminals are used more and more today for many different kinds of exams.
For an examination with very few applicants, you may be told to record your answers in the test booklet itself. Separate answer sheets are much more common. If this separate answer sheet is to be scored by machine – and this is often the case – it is highly important that you mark your answers correctly in order to get credit.

An electronic scoring machine is often used in civil service offices because of the speed with which papers can be scored. Machine-scored answer sheets must be marked with a pencil, which will be given to you. This pencil has a high graphite content which responds to the electronic scoring machine. As a matter of fact, stray dots may register as answers, so do not let your pencil rest on the answer sheet while you are pondering the correct answer. Also, if your pencil lead breaks or is otherwise defective, ask for another.

Since the answer sheet will be dropped in a slot in the scoring machine, be careful not to bend the corners or get the paper crumpled.

The answer sheet normally has five vertical columns of numbers, with 30 numbers to a column. These numbers correspond to the question numbers in your test booklet. After each number, going across the page are four or five pairs of dotted lines. These short dotted lines have small letters or numbers above them. The first two pairs may also have a "T" or "F" above the letters. This indicates that the first two pairs only are to be used if the questions are of the true-false type. If the questions are multiple choice, disregard the "T" and "F" and pay attention only to the small letters or numbers.

Answer your questions in the manner of the sample that follows:

32. The largest city in the United States is
    A. Washington, D.C.
    B. New York City
    C. Chicago
    D. Detroit
    E. San Francisco

1) Choose the answer you think is best. (New York City is the largest, so "B" is correct.)
2) Find the row of dotted lines numbered the same as the question you are answering. (Find row number 32)
3) Find the pair of dotted lines corresponding to the answer. (Find the pair of lines under the mark "B.")
4) Make a solid black mark between the dotted lines.

VI. BEFORE THE TEST

Common sense will help you find procedures to follow to get ready for an examination. Too many of us, however, overlook these sensible measures. Indeed, nervousness and fatigue have been found to be the most serious reasons why applicants fail to do their best on civil service tests. Here is a list of reminders:

- Begin your preparation early – Don't wait until the last minute to go scurrying around for books and materials or to find out what the position is all about.
- Prepare continuously – An hour a night for a week is better than an all-night cram session. This has been definitely established. What is more, a night a week for a month will return better dividends than crowding your study into a shorter period of time.
- Locate the place of the exam – You have been sent a notice telling you when and where to report for the examination. If the location is in a different town or otherwise unfamiliar to you, it would be well to inquire the best route and learn something about the building.
- Relax the night before the test – Allow your mind to rest. Do not study at all that night. Plan some mild recreation or diversion; then go to bed early and get a good night's sleep.
- Get up early enough to make a leisurely trip to the place for the test – This way unforeseen events, traffic snarls, unfamiliar buildings, etc. will not upset you.
- Dress comfortably – A written test is not a fashion show. You will be known by number and not by name, so wear something comfortable.

- Leave excess paraphernalia at home – Shopping bags and odd bundles will get in your way. You need bring only the items mentioned in the official notice you received; usually everything you need is provided. Do not bring reference books to the exam. They will only confuse those last minutes and be taken away from you when in the test room.
- Arrive somewhat ahead of time – If because of transportation schedules you must get there very early, bring a newspaper or magazine to take your mind off yourself while waiting.
- Locate the examination room – When you have found the proper room, you will be directed to the seat or part of the room where you will sit. Sometimes you are given a sheet of instructions to read while you are waiting. Do not fill out any forms until you are told to do so; just read them and be prepared.
- Relax and prepare to listen to the instructions
- If you have any physical problem that may keep you from doing your best, be sure to tell the test administrator. If you are sick or in poor health, you really cannot do your best on the exam. You can come back and take the test some other time.

VII. AT THE TEST

The day of the test is here and you have the test booklet in your hand. The temptation to get going is very strong. Caution! There is more to success than knowing the right answers. You must know how to identify your papers and understand variations in the type of short-answer question used in this particular examination. Follow these suggestions for maximum results from your efforts:

1) Cooperate with the monitor

The test administrator has a duty to create a situation in which you can be as much at ease as possible. He will give instructions, tell you when to begin, check to see that you are marking your answer sheet correctly, and so on. He is not there to guard you, although he will see that your competitors do not take unfair advantage. He wants to help you do your best.

2) Listen to all instructions

Don't jump the gun! Wait until you understand all directions. In most civil service tests you get more time than you need to answer the questions. So don't be in a hurry. Read each word of instructions until you clearly understand the meaning. Study the examples, listen to all announcements and follow directions. Ask questions if you do not understand what to do.

3) Identify your papers

Civil service exams are usually identified by number only. You will be assigned a number; you must not put your name on your test papers. Be sure to copy your number correctly. Since more than one exam may be given, copy your exact examination title.

4) Plan your time

Unless you are told that a test is a "speed" or "rate of work" test, speed itself is usually not important. Time enough to answer all the questions will be provided, but this does not mean that you have all day. An overall time limit has been set. Divide the total time (in minutes) by the number of questions to determine the approximate time you have for each question.

5) Do not linger over difficult questions

If you come across a difficult question, mark it with a paper clip (useful to have along) and come back to it when you have been through the booklet. One caution if you do this – be sure to skip a number on your answer sheet as well. Check often to be sure that you have not lost your place and that you are marking in the row numbered the same as the question you are answering.

6) Read the questions

Be sure you know what the question asks! Many capable people are unsuccessful because they failed to *read* the questions correctly.

7) Answer all questions

Unless you have been instructed that a penalty will be deducted for incorrect answers, it is better to guess than to omit a question.

8) Speed tests

It is often better NOT to guess on speed tests. It has been found that on timed tests people are tempted to spend the last few seconds before time is called in marking answers at random – without even reading them – in the hope of picking up a few extra points. To discourage this practice, the instructions may warn you that your score will be "corrected" for guessing. That is, a penalty will be applied. The incorrect answers will be deducted from the correct ones, or some other penalty formula will be used.

9) Review your answers

If you finish before time is called, go back to the questions you guessed or omitted to give them further thought. Review other answers if you have time.

10) Return your test materials

If you are ready to leave before others have finished or time is called, take ALL your materials to the monitor and leave quietly. Never take any test material with you. The monitor can discover whose papers are not complete, and taking a test booklet may be grounds for disqualification.

VIII. EXAMINATION TECHNIQUES

1) Read the general instructions carefully. These are usually printed on the first page of the exam booklet. As a rule, these instructions refer to the timing of the examination; the fact that you should not start work until the signal and must stop work at a signal, etc. If there are any *special* instructions, such as a choice of questions to be answered, make sure that you note this instruction carefully.

2) When you are ready to start work on the examination, that is as soon as the signal has been given, read the instructions to each question booklet, underline any key words or phrases, such as *least, best, outline, describe* and the like. In this way you will tend to answer as requested rather than discover on reviewing your paper that you *listed without describing*, that you selected the *worst* choice rather than the *best* choice, etc.

3) If the examination is of the objective or multiple-choice type – that is, each question will also give a series of possible answers: A, B, C or D, and you are called upon to select the best answer and write the letter next to that answer on your answer paper – it is advisable to start answering each question in turn. There may be anywhere from 50 to 100 such questions in the three or four hours allotted and you can see how much time would be taken if you read through all the questions before beginning to answer any. Furthermore, if you come across a question or group of questions which you know would be difficult to answer, it would undoubtedly affect your handling of all the other questions.

4) If the examination is of the essay type and contains but a few questions, it is a moot point as to whether you should read all the questions before starting to answer any one. Of course, if you are given a choice – say five out of seven and the like – then it is essential to read all the questions so you can eliminate the two that are most difficult. If, however, you are asked to answer all the questions, there may be danger in trying to answer the easiest one first because you may find that you will spend too much time on it. The best technique is to answer the first question, then proceed to the second, etc.

5) Time your answers. Before the exam begins, write down the time it started, then add the time allowed for the examination and write down the time it must be completed, then divide the time available somewhat as follows:
    - If 3-1/2 hours are allowed, that would be 210 minutes. If you have 80 objective-type questions, that would be an average of 2-1/2 minutes per question. Allow yourself no more than 2 minutes per question, or a total of 160 minutes, which will permit about 50 minutes to review.
    - If for the time allotment of 210 minutes there are 7 essay questions to answer, that would average about 30 minutes a question. Give yourself only 25 minutes per question so that you have about 35 minutes to review.

6) The most important instruction is to *read each question* and make sure you know what is wanted. The second most important instruction is to *time yourself properly* so that you answer every question. The third most important instruction is to *answer every question*. Guess if you have to but include something for each question. Remember that you will receive no credit for a blank and will probably receive some credit if you write something in answer to an essay question. If you guess a letter – say "B" for a multiple-choice question – you may have guessed right. If you leave a blank as an answer to a multiple-choice question, the examiners may respect your feelings but it will not add a point to your score. Some exams may penalize you for wrong answers, so in such cases *only*, you may not want to guess unless you have some basis for your answer.

7) Suggestions
    a. Objective-type questions
        1. Examine the question booklet for proper sequence of pages and questions
        2. Read all instructions carefully
        3. Skip any question which seems too difficult; return to it after all other questions have been answered
        4. Apportion your time properly; do not spend too much time on any single question or group of questions

5. Note and underline key words – *all, most, fewest, least, best, worst, same, opposite,* etc.
6. Pay particular attention to negatives
7. Note unusual option, e.g., unduly long, short, complex, different or similar in content to the body of the question
8. Observe the use of "hedging" words – *probably, may, most likely,* etc.
9. Make sure that your answer is put next to the same number as the question
10. Do not second-guess unless you have good reason to believe the second answer is definitely more correct
11. Cross out original answer if you decide another answer is more accurate; do not erase until you are ready to hand your paper in
12. Answer all questions; guess unless instructed otherwise
13. Leave time for review

   b. Essay questions
1. Read each question carefully
2. Determine exactly what is wanted. Underline key words or phrases.
3. Decide on outline or paragraph answer
4. Include many different points and elements unless asked to develop any one or two points or elements
5. Show impartiality by giving pros and cons unless directed to select one side only
6. Make and write down any assumptions you find necessary to answer the questions
7. Watch your English, grammar, punctuation and choice of words
8. Time your answers; don't crowd material

8) Answering the essay question

Most essay questions can be answered by framing the specific response around several key words or ideas. Here are a few such key words or ideas:

M's: manpower, materials, methods, money, management
P's: purpose, program, policy, plan, procedure, practice, problems, pitfalls, personnel, public relations

   a. Six basic steps in handling problems:
1. Preliminary plan and background development
2. Collect information, data and facts
3. Analyze and interpret information, data and facts
4. Analyze and develop solutions as well as make recommendations
5. Prepare report and sell recommendations
6. Install recommendations and follow up effectiveness

   b. Pitfalls to avoid
1. *Taking things for granted* – A statement of the situation does not necessarily imply that each of the elements is necessarily true; for example, a complaint may be invalid and biased so that all that can be taken for granted is that a complaint has been registered

2. *Considering only one side of a situation* – Wherever possible, indicate several alternatives and then point out the reasons you selected the best one
3. *Failing to indicate follow up* – Whenever your answer indicates action on your part, make certain that you will take proper follow-up action to see how successful your recommendations, procedures or actions turn out to be
4. *Taking too long in answering any single question* – Remember to time your answers properly

IX. AFTER THE TEST

Scoring procedures differ in detail among civil service jurisdictions although the general principles are the same. Whether the papers are hand-scored or graded by machine we have described, they are nearly always graded by number. That is, the person who marks the paper knows only the number – never the name – of the applicant. Not until all the papers have been graded will they be matched with names. If other tests, such as training and experience or oral interview ratings have been given, scores will be combined. Different parts of the examination usually have different weights. For example, the written test might count 60 percent of the final grade, and a rating of training and experience 40 percent. In many jurisdictions, veterans will have a certain number of points added to their grades.

After the final grade has been determined, the names are placed in grade order and an eligible list is established. There are various methods for resolving ties between those who get the same final grade – probably the most common is to place first the name of the person whose application was received first. Job offers are made from the eligible list in the order the names appear on it. You will be notified of your grade and your rank as soon as all these computations have been made. This will be done as rapidly as possible.

People who are found to meet the requirements in the announcement are called "eligibles." Their names are put on a list of eligible candidates. An eligible's chances of getting a job depend on how high he stands on this list and how fast agencies are filling jobs from the list.

When a job is to be filled from a list of eligibles, the agency asks for the names of people on the list of eligibles for that job. When the civil service commission receives this request, it sends to the agency the names of the three people highest on this list. Or, if the job to be filled has specialized requirements, the office sends the agency the names of the top three persons who meet these requirements from the general list.

The appointing officer makes a choice from among the three people whose names were sent to him. If the selected person accepts the appointment, the names of the others are put back on the list to be considered for future openings.

That is the rule in hiring from all kinds of eligible lists, whether they are for typist, carpenter, chemist, or something else. For every vacancy, the appointing officer has his choice of any one of the top three eligibles on the list. This explains why the person whose name is on top of the list sometimes does not get an appointment when some of the persons lower on the list do. If the appointing officer chooses the second or third eligible, the No. 1 eligible does not get a job at once, but stays on the list until he is appointed or the list is terminated.

X. HOW TO PASS THE INTERVIEW TEST

The examination for which you applied requires an oral interview test. You have already taken the written test and you are now being called for the interview test – the final part of the formal examination.

You may think that it is not possible to prepare for an interview test and that there are no procedures to follow during an interview. Our purpose is to point out some things you can do in advance that will help you and some good rules to follow and pitfalls to avoid while you are being interviewed.

What is an interview supposed to test?

The written examination is designed to test the technical knowledge and competence of the candidate; the oral is designed to evaluate intangible qualities, not readily measured otherwise, and to establish a list showing the relative fitness of each candidate – as measured against his competitors – for the position sought. Scoring is not on the basis of "right" and "wrong," but on a sliding scale of values ranging from "not passable" to "outstanding." As a matter of fact, it is possible to achieve a relatively low score without a single "incorrect" answer because of evident weakness in the qualities being measured.

Occasionally, an examination may consist entirely of an oral test – either an individual or a group oral. In such cases, information is sought concerning the technical knowledges and abilities of the candidate, since there has been no written examination for this purpose. More commonly, however, an oral test is used to supplement a written examination.

Who conducts interviews?

The composition of oral boards varies among different jurisdictions. In nearly all, a representative of the personnel department serves as chairman. One of the members of the board may be a representative of the department in which the candidate would work. In some cases, "outside experts" are used, and, frequently, a businessman or some other representative of the general public is asked to serve. Labor and management or other special groups may be represented. The aim is to secure the services of experts in the appropriate field.

However the board is composed, it is a good idea (and not at all improper or unethical) to ascertain in advance of the interview who the members are and what groups they represent. When you are introduced to them, you will have some idea of their backgrounds and interests, and at least you will not stutter and stammer over their names.

What should be done before the interview?

While knowledge about the board members is useful and takes some of the surprise element out of the interview, there is other preparation which is more substantive. It *is* possible to prepare for an oral interview – in several ways:

1) Keep a copy of your application and review it carefully before the interview

This may be the only document before the oral board, and the starting point of the interview. Know what education and experience you have listed there, and the sequence and dates of all of it. Sometimes the board will ask you to review the highlights of your experience for them; you should not have to hem and haw doing it.

2) Study the class specification and the examination announcement

Usually, the oral board has one or both of these to guide them. The qualities, characteristics or knowledges required by the position sought are stated in these documents. They offer valuable clues as to the nature of the oral interview. For example, if the job involves supervisory responsibilities, the announcement will usually indicate that knowledge of modern supervisory methods and the qualifications of the candidate as a supervisor will be tested. If so, you can expect such questions, frequently in the form of a hypothetical situation which you are expected to solve. NEVER go into an oral without knowledge of the duties and responsibilities of the job you seek.

3) Think through each qualification required

Try to visualize the kind of questions you would ask if you were a board member. How well could you answer them? Try especially to appraise your own knowledge and background in each area, *measured against the job sought*, and identify any areas in which you are weak. Be critical and realistic – do not flatter yourself.

4) Do some general reading in areas in which you feel you may be weak

For example, if the job involves supervision and your past experience has NOT, some general reading in supervisory methods and practices, particularly in the field of human relations, might be useful. Do NOT study agency procedures or detailed manuals. The oral board will be testing your understanding and capacity, not your memory.

5) Get a good night's sleep and watch your general health and mental attitude

You will want a clear head at the interview. Take care of a cold or any other minor ailment, and of course, no hangovers.

What should be done on the day of the interview?

Now comes the day of the interview itself. Give yourself plenty of time to get there. Plan to arrive somewhat ahead of the scheduled time, particularly if your appointment is in the fore part of the day. If a previous candidate fails to appear, the board might be ready for you a bit early. By early afternoon an oral board is almost invariably behind schedule if there are many candidates, and you may have to wait. Take along a book or magazine to read, or your application to review, but leave any extraneous material in the waiting room when you go in for your interview. In any event, relax and compose yourself.

The matter of dress is important. The board is forming impressions about you – from your experience, your manners, your attitude, and your appearance. Give your personal appearance careful attention. Dress your best, but not your flashiest. Choose conservative, appropriate clothing, and be sure it is immaculate. This is a business interview, and your appearance should indicate that you regard it as such. Besides, being well groomed and properly dressed will help boost your confidence.

Sooner or later, someone will call your name and escort you into the interview room. *This is it.* From here on you are on your own. It is too late for any more preparation. But remember, you asked for this opportunity to prove your fitness, and you are here because your request was granted.

What happens when you go in?

The usual sequence of events will be as follows: The clerk (who is often the board stenographer) will introduce you to the chairman of the oral board, who will introduce you to the other members of the board. Acknowledge the introductions before you sit down. Do not be surprised if you find a microphone facing you or a stenotypist sitting by. Oral interviews are usually recorded in the event of an appeal or other review.

Usually the chairman of the board will open the interview by reviewing the highlights of your education and work experience from your application – primarily for the benefit of the other members of the board, as well as to get the material into the record. Do not interrupt or comment unless there is an error or significant misinterpretation; if that is the case, do not hesitate. But do not quibble about insignificant matters. Also, he will usually ask you some question about your education, experience or your present job – partly to get you to start talking and to establish the interviewing "rapport." He may start the actual questioning, or turn it over to one of the other members. Frequently, each member undertakes the questioning on a particular area, one in which he is perhaps most competent, so you can expect each member to participate in the examination. Because time is limited, you may also expect some rather abrupt switches in the direction the questioning takes, so do not be upset by it. Normally, a board member will not pursue a single line of questioning unless he discovers a particular strength or weakness.

After each member has participated, the chairman will usually ask whether any member has any further questions, then will ask you if you have anything you wish to add. Unless you are expecting this question, it may floor you. Worse, it may start you off on an extended, extemporaneous speech. The board is not usually seeking more information. The question is principally to offer you a last opportunity to present further qualifications or to indicate that you have nothing to add. So, if you feel that a significant qualification or characteristic has been overlooked, it is proper to point it out in a sentence or so. Do not compliment the board on the thoroughness of their examination – they have been sketchy, and you know it. If you wish, merely say, "No thank you, I have nothing further to add." This is a point where you can "talk yourself out" of a good impression or fail to present an important bit of information. Remember, *you close the interview yourself*.

The chairman will then say, "That is all, Mr. _____, thank you." Do not be startled; the interview is over, and quicker than you think. Thank him, gather your belongings and take your leave. Save your sigh of relief for the other side of the door.

How to put your best foot forward

Throughout this entire process, you may feel that the board individually and collectively is trying to pierce your defenses, seek out your hidden weaknesses and embarrass and confuse you. Actually, this is not true. They are obliged to make an appraisal of your qualifications for the job you are seeking, and they want to see you in your best light. Remember, they must interview all candidates and a non-cooperative candidate may become a failure in spite of their best efforts to bring out his qualifications. Here are 15 suggestions that will help you:

1) Be natural – Keep your attitude confident, not cocky

If you are not confident that you can do the job, do not expect the board to be. Do not apologize for your weaknesses, try to bring out your strong points. The board is interested in a positive, not negative, presentation. Cockiness will antagonize any board member and make him wonder if you are covering up a weakness by a false show of strength.

2) Get comfortable, but don't lounge or sprawl

Sit erectly but not stiffly. A careless posture may lead the board to conclude that you are careless in other things, or at least that you are not impressed by the importance of the occasion. Either conclusion is natural, even if incorrect. Do not fuss with your clothing, a pencil or an ashtray. Your hands may occasionally be useful to emphasize a point; do not let them become a point of distraction.

3) Do not wisecrack or make small talk

This is a serious situation, and your attitude should show that you consider it as such. Further, the time of the board is limited – they do not want to waste it, and neither should you.

4) Do not exaggerate your experience or abilities

In the first place, from information in the application or other interviews and sources, the board may know more about you than you think. Secondly, you probably will not get away with it. An experienced board is rather adept at spotting such a situation, so do not take the chance.

5) If you know a board member, do not make a point of it, yet do not hide it

Certainly you are not fooling him, and probably not the other members of the board. Do not try to take advantage of your acquaintanceship – it will probably do you little good.

6) Do not dominate the interview

Let the board do that. They will give you the clues – do not assume that you have to do all the talking. Realize that the board has a number of questions to ask you, and do not try to take up all the interview time by showing off your extensive knowledge of the answer to the first one.

7) Be attentive

You only have 20 minutes or so, and you should keep your attention at its sharpest throughout. When a member is addressing a problem or question to you, give him your undivided attention. Address your reply principally to him, but do not exclude the other board members.

8) Do not interrupt

A board member may be stating a problem for you to analyze. He will ask you a question when the time comes. Let him state the problem, and wait for the question.

9) Make sure you understand the question

Do not try to answer until you are sure what the question is. If it is not clear, restate it in your own words or ask the board member to clarify it for you. However, do not haggle about minor elements.

10) Reply promptly but not hastily

A common entry on oral board rating sheets is "candidate responded readily," or "candidate hesitated in replies." Respond as promptly and quickly as you can, but do not jump to a hasty, ill-considered answer.

11) Do not be peremptory in your answers

A brief answer is proper – but do not fire your answer back. That is a losing game from your point of view. The board member can probably ask questions much faster than you can answer them.

12) Do not try to create the answer you think the board member wants

He is interested in what kind of mind you have and how it works – not in playing games. Furthermore, he can usually spot this practice and will actually grade you down on it.

13) Do not switch sides in your reply merely to agree with a board member

Frequently, a member will take a contrary position merely to draw you out and to see if you are willing and able to defend your point of view. Do not start a debate, yet do not surrender a good position. If a position is worth taking, it is worth defending.

14) Do not be afraid to admit an error in judgment if you are shown to be wrong

The board knows that you are forced to reply without any opportunity for careful consideration. Your answer may be demonstrably wrong. If so, admit it and get on with the interview.

15) Do not dwell at length on your present job

The opening question may relate to your present assignment. Answer the question but do not go into an extended discussion. You are being examined for a *new* job, not your present one. As a matter of fact, try to phrase ALL your answers in terms of the job for which you are being examined.

Basis of Rating

Probably you will forget most of these "do's" and "don'ts" when you walk into the oral interview room. Even remembering them all will not ensure you a passing grade. Perhaps you did not have the qualifications in the first place. But remembering them will help you to put your best foot forward, without treading on the toes of the board members.

Rumor and popular opinion to the contrary notwithstanding, an oral board wants you to make the best appearance possible. They know you are under pressure – but they also want to see how you respond to it as a guide to what your reaction would be under the pressures of the job you seek. They will be influenced by the degree of poise you display, the personal traits you show and the manner in which you respond.

ABOUT THIS BOOK

This book contains tests divided into Examination Sections. Go through each test, answering every question in the margin. We have also attached a sample answer sheet at the back of the book that can be removed and used. At the end of each test look at the answer key and check your answers. On the ones you got wrong, look at the right answer choice and learn. Do not fill in the answers first. Do not memorize the questions and answers, but understand the answer and principles involved. On your test, the questions will likely be different from the samples. Questions are changed and new ones added. If you understand these past questions you should have success with any changes that arise. Tests may consist of several types of questions. We have additional books on each subject should more study be advisable or necessary for you. Finally, the more you study, the better prepared you will be. This book is intended to be the last thing you study before you walk into the examination room. Prior study of relevant texts is also recommended. NLC publishes some of these in our Fundamental Series. Knowledge and good sense are important factors in passing your exam. Good luck also helps. So now study this Passbook, absorb the material contained within and take that knowledge into the examination. Then do your best to pass that exam.

EXAMINATION SECTION

EXAMINATION SECTION
TEST 1

DIRECTIONS: Each question or incomplete statement is followed by several suggested answers or completions. Select the one that BEST answers the question or completes the Statement. *PRINT THE LETTER OF THE CORRECT ANSWER IN THE SPACE AT THE RIGHT.*

1. A vandal throws a stone and injures a raliroad porter who is working at an elevated train station. When the porter's assistant station supervisor submits a supervisory accident report for the accident to his supervisor for approval, the latter should make sure that the proper category for RESPONSIBILITY has been checked off.
   The proper RESPONSIBILITY category that should be checked for this accident is

   A. Control of Other Than Company or Employee
   B. Impractical to Control
   C. Supervision
   D. Employee

   1._____

2. Assume that you are a station supervisor and you notice that the accident rate for a particular heavy duty cleaning gang has increased to an unacceptable level.
   Of the following, the BEST method of handling this problem is to tell the assistant station supervisor in charge of this gang

   A. to watch his men more closely when they work and to correct any unsafe work habits they may have
   B. that the accident rate for his gang is too high and that it reflects poorly on the work record of his gang
   C. that he must severely penalize those men who are most accident prone in order to set an example for the others in the gang
   D. to assign the easiest work tasks to those men who have the most accidents

   2._____

3. Assume that your superior gives you orders to carry out a special assignment. However, you believe there is an error in his orders.
   Which one of the following statements BEST describes the action you should take in this situation?

   A. Carry out the orders exactly as given to you
   B. Carry out the orders, but modify them to correct the error
   C. Delay carrying out the orders and give your superior a chance to detect the error himself
   D. Point out the error to your superior before carrying out the orders

   3._____

4. A work sheet for a booth audit has the readings shown below for four turnstiles:

Turnstile No.	Opening Readings	Readings For Audit
1	26178	26291
2	65489	65752
3	72267	72312
4	45965	46199

   With a fare of $2.50, what is the cash value of the total difference between the Opening Readings and the Readings for Audit for the four turnstiles?

   4._____

1

A. A. $1,587.50   B. $1,632.50   C. $1,637.50   D. $1,687.50

5. When an employee is suspected of being under the influence of alcohol, a member of supervision must make out a written report of the incident. This supervisor should include in his report the answer to certain questions that he has asked the employee. Following are *four* possible questions that the supervisor might ask the employee:
    I. What kind of beverage did you drink?
    II. How much alcohol did the beverage contain?
    III. When did you drink this beverage?
    IV. How much of the beverage did you drink?
   Which *one* of the following choices lists *only* those of the above questions that must be asked for the preparation of the written report?

   A. I, II, and III   B. I, III, and IV
   C. I, II, and IV   D. II, III, and IV

6. Following are *four* statements relating to collection train operations, which may or may not be correct:
    I. The assistant station supervisor in charge of a collection train must follow the prepared schedule of revenue collections at all times and is not authorized to deviate from it.
    II. The checking of bags delivered to the collection train will be done after the count of bags to the tally clerks has been completed, and while the train is moving from one station to another.
    III. The tally clerk will arrange the railroad clerks' daily reports in booth and trick order, and he will personally deliver these reports to the representative of the revenue department on duty in the revenue room.
    IV. The tally clerk of each revenue train will check keys, dials and related equipment received from collection parties, and will see to the disposition of these items according to scheduled procedure, unless otherwise directed by an authorized supervisor.
   Which of the following choices lists *all* the above statements that are correct and *none* that is incorrect?

   A. I and II   B. I, II, and III
   C. II, III, and IV   D. III and IV

Questions 7-10.

DIRECTIONS: Questions 7 to 10 require computing basic schedule working time for certain specified tasks for porters assigned to one station. The questions apply to an average station for which the statistics are as follows:

STATION STATISTICS

Tile: 3,747 linear feet (average height of 9 1/2 feet)

No. of Entrance Stairways: 7

No. of Rolled Platform Columns: Northbound 72,
                                  Southbound 76

Active Floor Area: Northbound Platform 12,345 sq. ft.
                     Southbound Platform 12,987 sq. ft.

7. The total computed time required to sweep all the entrance stairways daily from Monday through Friday is, *most nearly*, _____ hour(s).

   A. 1 B. 4 3/4 C. 5 1/2 D. 6

8. If all the columns in the station must be cleaned once in a period of 4 weeks, the total computed time that should be allotted to the cleaning of columns each week is, *most nearly*, _____ hours.

   A. 6 1/4 B. 7 1/4 C. 8 D. 10 1/4

9. The total weekly computed time for sweeping the active floor area twice a week is, *most nearly*, _____ hours.

   A. 4 1/2 B. 6 C. 8 3/4 D. 9 1/4

10. As a major duty, the tile must be cleaned once in a period of 4 weeks. Therefore, the total computed time for cleaning tile each week is closest to _____ hours.

    A. 18.7 B. 23.4 C. 27.2 D. 93.6

11. Assume that a new procedure affecting railroad clerks is to be put into operation immediately. At a staff conference attended by station supervisors and the chief of operations concerning this new procedure, you had objected to it because you believed it would cause a reduction in efficiency, and you thought the present procedure was adequate. Of the following, the BEST course of action for you to take should be to instruct your subordinates to

    A. follow the new procedure, but indicate to them that you do not like it
    B. follow the procedure which they think is best
    C. avoid following the new procedure until the next scheduled staff conference
    D. follow the new procedure and maintain careful notes on how it works

12. Following are *four* statements relating to procedures for unusual occurrences and the preparation of related reports, which may or may not be correct:
    I. At all times a prompt report of every unusual occurrence should be made by telephone to the field office
    II. The telephone report of the occurrence should include the time, the place, and a concise statement of the circumstances and action taken, including the names and addresses of passengers and the names and badge numbers of employees and police officers involved
    III. If the occurrence is of an emergency nature, the field office should be notified first and the police office and station department office notified afterwards.
    IV. Train whistle signals for help, which consist of one short-one long- one short- one long blast, should be given immediate response by station department employees.

    Which of the following choices lists *all* of the above statements that are correct and *none* that is incorrect?

    A. I and II B. II C. III D. III and IV

13. Following are *four* statements relating to the duties of collecting agents, which may or may not be correct:
    I. A collecting agent may not reveal a safe combination except if he has received a verbal order to do so by the assistant general superintendent or his authorized representative.
    II. Unless specifically excused, each collecting agent while on duty will wear his uniform cap and badge and will also carry his revolver permit on his person.
    III. Revolvers will be issued to collecting agents in the presence of either the transit patrolman or the assistant station supervisor in charge of revenue collections at designated points and returned in the same manner.
    IV. No collecting agent should have his revolver or badge in his possession while off duty.

    Which one of the following choices lists all of the above statements that are correct and *none* that is incorrect?

    A. I and II
    B. II and III
    C. II and IV
    D. III and IV

14. Following are *four* statements relating to time card rules, which may or may not be correct:
    I. The entering of time worked by one employee on another employee's time card is forbidden.
    II. Assistant station supervisors are authorized to make notations on employees' time cards in order to draw the attention of the timekeeper to incorrect entries.
    III. Time cards for court attendance and trial board hearings should be forwarded to the station department office for verification and signature.
    IV. Per annum employees are required to submit their time cards at designated locations on the last day of each bi-weekly pay period.

    Which one of the following choices lists *all* of the above statements that are correct and *none* that is incorrect?

    A. I, II, and III
    B. I, III, and IV
    C. I, II, III, and IV
    D. II, III, and IV

15. As a rule, the stairs at all stations are numbered consecutively beginning at the _____ end.

    A. southeast
    B. southwest
    C. northeast
    D. northwest

16. The type of construction *generally* used for sliding gates at stations is designated as _____ rail.

    A. *E*
    B. *F*
    C. *G*
    D. *H*

17. At 9:00 A.M. you are requested by your superior to investigate a situation which has arisen. Turnstiles at a certain station have been repeatedly vandalized over the past week causing a serious revenue loss to the authority and inconvenience to the public. You are told that this is an urgent job and that you must submit a written report to your superior by 5:00 P.M. of that day.
For the report to be of GREATEST immediate value to your superior, it should contain some of the following items:
   I. A brief statement of the problem
   II. A detailed description of the problem
   III. Detailed plans of the platform and station layout
   IV. An outline of possible practical alternate solutions
   V. Your recommended solution

Which of the following choices lists *only* those of the above items to be included in the report so that the report is of GREATEST immediate value to your superior?

A. I, III, and IV
B. I, III, and V
C. I, IV, and V
D. II, III, V

17.____

Questions 18-20.

DIRECTIONS: Questions 18 to 20 are based on the article shown below entitled *EMPLOYEE NEEDS*. Refer to this article when answering these questions.

EMPLOYEE NEEDS

The greatest waste in industry and in government may be that of human resources. This waste usually derives not from employees' unwillingness or inability, but from management's ineptness to meet the maintenance and motivational needs of employees. Maintenance needs refer to such needs as providing employees with safe places to work, written work rules, job security, adequate salary, employer sponsored social activities, and with knowledge of their role in the over-all framework of the organization. However, of greatest significance to employees are the motivational needs of job growth, achievement, responsibility and recognition.

Although employee dissatisfaction may stem from either poor maintenance or poor motivation factors, the outward manifestation of the dissatisfaction may be very much alike, i.e. negativism, complaints, deterioration of performance, and so forth. The improvement in the lighting of an employee's work area or raising his level of pay won't do much good if the source of the dissatisfaction is the absence of a meaningful assignment. By the same token, if an employee is dissatisfied with what he considers inequitable pay the introduction of additional challenge in his work may simply make matters worse.

It is relatively easy for an employee to express frustration by complaining about pay, wash room conditions, fringe benefits and so forth; but most people cannot easily express resentment in terms of the more abstract concepts concerning job growth, responsibility, and achievement.

It would be wrong to assume that there is no interaction between maintenance and motivational needs of employees. For example, conditions of high motivation often overshadow poor maintenance conditions. If an organization is in a period of strong growth and expansion, opportunities for job growth, responsibility, recognition and achievement are usually abundant, but the rapid growth may have outrun the upkeep of maintenance factors. In this situation, motivation may be high, but only if employees recognize the poor maintenance conditions as unavoidable and temporary. The subordination of maintenance factors cannot go on indefinitely, even with the highest motivation.

Both maintenance and motivation factors influence the behavior of all employees, but employees are not identical and, furthermore, the needs of any individual do not remain constant. However, a broad distinction can be made between employees who have a basic orientation toward maintenance factors and those with greater sensitivity toward motivation factors.

A highly maintenance-oriented individual, preoccupied with the factors peripheral to his job rather than the job itself, is more concerned with comfort than challenge. He does not get deeply involved with his work but does with the condition of his work area, toilet facilities and his time for going to lunch. By contrast, a strongly motivation-oriented employee is usually relatively indifferent to his surroundings and is caught up in the pursuit of work goals.

Fortunately, there are few people who are either exclusively maintenance-oriented or purely motivation-oriented. The former would be deadwood in an organization, while the latter might trample on those around him in his pursuit to achieve his goals.

18. With respect to employee motivational and maintenance needs, the management policies of an organization which is growing rapidly will probably result

    A. more in meeting motivational needs rather than maintenance needs
    B. more in meeting maintenance needs rather than motivational needs
    C. in meeting both of these needs equally
    D. in increased effort to define the motivational and maintenance needs of its employees

19. In accordance with the above article, which of the following CANNOT be considered as an example of an employee maintenance need for railroad clerks?

    A. Providing more relief periods
    B. Providing fair salary increases at periodic intervals
    C. Increasing job responsibilities
    D. Increasing health insurance benefits

20. Most employees in an organization may be categorized as being interested in

    A. maintenance needs only
    B. motivational needs only
    C. both motivational and maintenance needs
    D. money only, to the exclusion of all other needs

KEY (CORRECT ANSWERS)

1. A
2. A
3. D
4. C
5. B

6. C
7. B
8. A
9. D
10. B

11. D
12. B
13. C
14. C
15. A

16. D
17. C
18. A
19. C
20. C

TEST 2

DIRECTIONS: Each question or incomplete statement is followed by several suggested answers or completions. Select the one that BEST answers the question or completes the Statement. *PRINT THE LETTER OF THE CORRECT ANSWER IN THE SPACE AT THE RIGHT.*

1. The following are possible actions that a railroad clerk could take: when a passenger tells him that he lost money in a malfunctioning vending machine:
    I. Close the coin slot on the vending machine
    II. List the name and address of the passenger on the prescribed form
    III. Refund the lost amount of money to the passenger
    IV. Notify the station department control desk

    Which of the following choices lists *all* the correct actions stated above that the railroad clerk should take?

    A. I and II
    B. I, II, and III
    C. I, II, and IV
    D. II and IV

2. Assume that 326 railroad porters will begin using a new type of disinfectant at certain stations as part of a test to determine the suitability of the disinfectant for authority use. If 14 ounces of undiluted disinfectant must be added to 3 gallons of water to make a satisfactory solution of the disinfectant and each porter is expected to use approximately 5 gallons of disinfectant solution each week, the amount of undiluted disinfectant needed for *all* the porters for a 6- week test is _____ ounces.

    A. 3890
    B. 4890
    C. 4990
    D. 5890

3. Below are *four* possible actions which may or may not be taken in dealing with snow or sleet storms in accordance with standard operating procedures:
    I. Superintendents and station supervisors will communicate with the assistant general superintendent or his designated alternate for any special assignments.
    II. Assistant station supervisors who do not have a telephone at home will be required to communicate with their field office for assignment and if no assignment is given they will report for their next regularly assigned tour of duty.
    III. When a storm is of such severity that assistance from the bureau of track and structures is required, the supervisor on duty in the station department office will make such request to the ranking official of the bureau of track and structures.
    IV. On elevated stations where there are open ties, snow may be thrown between the running rails if extreme care is used to prevent tripping of trains.

    Which of the following choices lists *all* of the above procedures that are correct and *none* that is incorrect?

    A. I and III
    B. II and III
    C. II and IV
    D. III and IV

4. If the total number of accidents to the public on authority property in May 2007 was 529 and in May 2008 was 585, the *percent increase* in accidents in May 2008 as compared to May 2007 is closest to

    A. 7%
    B. 9%
    C. 11%
    D. 13%

5. You are instructing a newly appointed assistant station supervisor on the procedures for making a semi-annual inspection of a concession on authority property.
   You should tell him that if the concession has NO cooking facilities, he should check whether the concessionaire has on his premises a _____ fire extinguisher.

   A. 2 lb. dry chemical
   B. 5 lb. dry chemical
   C. 2 1/2 gallon water-type pressurized
   D. 10 lb. capacity carbon dioxide

6. The repair of malfunctioning public address speakers in the vicinity of token booths is the responsibility of the

   A. telephone subdivision
   B. station department
   C. rapid transit operations department
   D. signal division

7. A wooden edging, level with the floor of a concrete platform and running its entire length, which is used to reduce the gap between the platform and a train is called a

   A. rubbing board   B. coping
   C. pantograph   D. slap rail

8. A railroad clerk, paid $11.48 an hour, works a 7:00 A.M. to 3:00 P.M. tour of duty Monday through Friday.
   What is his gross pay for a particular week if he is ordered to instruct a newly-appointed railroad clerk in the performance of his duties in his booth each day of that week during his tour?

   A. $482.16   B. $516.60   C. $533.82   D. $539.56

9. Assume that your superintendent has asked you to research a problem and to provide him with all the information necessary for him to arrive at a solution. In assembling this information you should be *especially* careful to give him *only* information which

   A. has been collected objectively
   B. will be consistent with previous information on this problem
   C. supports the present thinking of your superintendent
   D. in your judgment will provide the best solution to the problem

10. The following are possible supervisory practices which a station supervisor might employ to create a healthy climate for work, morale, and discipline among his subordinates:
    I. Tell subordinates that he will not answer questions which are covered by the book of rules
    II. Encourage subordinates to ask questions when in doubt about station department policies
    III. Praise subordinates in public, but reprimand them in private
    IV. Warn subordinates that they should feel guilty about making a mistake
    V. When a mistake is made, immediately institute disciplinary action regardless of the causes
    VI. If a subordinate makes a significant mistake, use the opportunity to teach him the correct procedure

Which one of the following choices contains *only* those of the above supervisory practices which are helpful for a station supervisor to follow in creating a healthy climate for work, morale, and discipline?

    A. I, II, and IV   B. I, IV, and V
    C. II, III, and VI   D. III, IV, and V

11. When formulating the annual operating budget in the station department, it is necessary to determine the number of man-days required to cover the various work programs. If the railroad porter's work program calls for 2,354 daily tours, 2,163 Saturday tours, and 1,980 Sunday tours (including holidays), then the number of man-days which are normally required to cover this one-year work program without taking into account vacation coverage is, *most nearly,*

    A. 730,000   B. 780,000   C. 830,000   D. 880,000

12. Assume that you are in charge of a field office. At the beginning of your tour on a particular day you are faced with the following *four* almost simultaneous situations:
    I. One of your railroad clerks has telephoned your assistant station supervisor and has asked that you return her call as soon as possible because she has a question about her daily fare report.
    II. One of your railroad porters at an elevated station has telephoned you to report that a small section of one of the concrete platforms has broken off and fallen to the street.
    III. A clerk from the chief of operations office has telephoned you and has requested you to complete and submit to them a special material utilization report immediately, since it is urgently needed at their office.
    IV. One of your assistant station supervisors gives you a written message regarding important information that you must use in the preparation of a statistical report covering emergency actions taken during the preceding month.

    Which one of the above four situations should you take care of FIRST?

        A. I   B. II   C. III   D. IV

13. A railroad clerk complains to you that a certain newly appointed assistant station supervisor under your supervision has been making rude and insulting comments to her about her work.
    The following are offered as possible actions that you could consider taking in this matter:
    I. Interview the railroad clerk personally and obtain as many details of the alleged incidents as possible
    II. Ask the railroad clerk to be patient with the assistant station supervisor as he is still nervous about his new duties
    III. Tell the railroad clerk to keep a daily log of her encounters with this assistant station supervisor and make a report to you in one week
    IV. Summon the assistant station supervisor and ask him for an explanation
    V. Summon the railroad clerk and explain that this is not your concern but more properly a matter for her union representative

    Which of the following choices lists the BEST of the above actions to be taken in handling this matter?

        A. I and II   B. I and IV   C. II and III   D. IV and V

14. You have been assigned to evaluate three different new cleansing powders for tile surfaces and to recommend the use of one of them for the station department. In your investigation you have determined that all of the cleansers can do equally satisfactory jobs. Therefore, your recommendation of the cleanser to use should be based PRIMARILY on which one costs *least* per

  A. pound
  B. square foot of tile cleaned
  C. gallon of water used
  D. package

14.____

15. A station supervisor leaves written instructions in connection with a work matter for one of his assistant station supervisors, and, in these instructions, he clearly delegates authority to the latter to supervise the job. In this situation, it would be BEST if the assistant station supervisor

  A. used his delegated authority to make any changes in the scope of the job and its related activities that he feels are necessary
  B. notifies the station supervisor each time he uses his delegated authority on the job
  C. goes to the station supervisor frequently to check out details of the job as it progresses
  D. goes to the station supervisor only if there are unusual problems

15.____

16. The station supervisor in charge of a collection train must make sure that the collection train, and, in particular, the car in which the revenue is carried, is NEVER left without *at least* _____ armed guards.

  A. one B. two C. three D. four

16.____

17. When a train derailment or other major emergency occurs, the PRIMARY source for information to the news media about details of the incident should be the

  A. director of public information and community relations
  B. executive officer, operations and maintenance
  C. emergency press center
  D. station department office

17.____

18. Making supervisory decisions should be based on sound, problem-solving principles. Following are five principles which you might consider in trying to solve difficult problems:

  I. Make sure you understand the problems you are expected to solve
  II. Make sure you have some idea of possible solutions before you start working on the problems
  III. Review the results of past decisions on similar problems to provide helpful precedents
  IV. Consider the possible solutions to the problems without taking into account their consequences
  V. Call on your associates for help, especially those with experience in the areas involved

Which of the following choices lists *all* of the above principles which are correct and *none* that is incorrect?

  A. I, III, and V   B. I, II, and III
  C. II, IV, and V   D. III, IV, and V

18.____

19. *A no clearance area* in the subway is indicated by a sign that has diagonal stripes that are colored *alternately*

   A. red and white
   B. red and black
   C. black and white
   D. black and yellow

20. The operation and maintenance of station department facilities is a continuing process. A station supervisor should seek ways to improve the efficiency of those operations which he supervises by such means as changing established methods and procedures that appear wasteful and inefficient.
   The following are possible courses of action which could be taken when changing established methods and procedures:
       I. Make changes only when your subordinates agree to them
       II. Make changes quickly and quietly in order to avoid dissent
       III. Secure expert guidance before instituting unfamiliar procedures
       IV. Standardize operations which are performed on a continuing basis
       V. Discuss changes with your superintendent before putting them into practice
   Which of the following choices lists *only* those actions stated above which are useful when changing established methods or procedures?

   A. I, II, and III
   B. I, II, II, and V
   C. II, III, and IV
   D. III, IV, and V

21. A location in the subway having a blue light should normally have which of the following types of equipment?
   An emergency alarm box

   A. *only*
   B. *and* a telephone only
   C. *and* a fire extinguisher only
   D. a telephone and a fire extinguisher

22. The train whistle or horn signal which is meant to be an alarm to persons on a station platform consists of _____ blasts.

   A. one long
   B. two long
   C. two short
   D. a succession of short

23. When removing bags of coins from the reserve supply, railroad clerks are directed to place on sale the bag with the

   A. least number of coins
   B. most number of coins
   C. most recent date
   D. oldest date

24. A railroad clerk, paid $10.80 an hour, works a 7:00 A.M. to 3:00 P.M. tour of duty Monday through Friday.
   What is his gross pay for a particular day on which he is required to attend a class on a new station department procedure for two hours after the completion of his tour of duty?

   A. $86.40
   B. $108.00
   C. $118.80
   D. $129.60

25. After using up all time credited to him, a railroad clerk who is eligible to receive 60% sick pay may receive this benefit if he is off sick for a minimum of _____ or more consecutive working days. 25.____

    A. 9   B. 14   C. 21   D. 25

KEY (CORRECT ANSWERS)

1. C		11. C
2. B		12. B
3. D		13. B
4. C		14. B
5. C		15. D
6. A		16. B
7. A		17. C
8. B		18. A
9. A		19. A
10. C		20. D

21. D
22. D
23. D
24. C
25. A

EXAMINATION SECTION
TEST 1

DIRECTIONS: Each question or incomplete statement is followed by several suggested answers or completions. Select the one that BEST answers the question or completes the statement. *PRINT THE LETTER OF THE CORRECT ANSWER IN THE SPACE AT THE RIGHT.*

Questions 1-7.

DIRECTIONS: Questions 1 to 7 are based on the portion of a COMBINED RAILROAD CLERKS DAILY FARE REPORT shown on the next page. Some of the computed entries in this report may not be mathematically correct. In answering the questions, you are to determine the accuracy of certain computed entries. You are to assume that all entries which are not computed on this report but which are copies or transferred from another source, such as OPENING readings and TOKENS RECEIVED entries, are correct. NO OTHER ASSUMPTIONS ABOUT THE CORRECTNESS OF ENTRIES CAN BE MADE.

1. For John Doe's tour of duty, the entries made on line T in the OPENING and CLOSING columns are 199780 and 202628, respectively.
   Select the statement below which BEST describes the accuracy of these totals.

   A. The total in the OPENING column is incorrect.
   B. The total in the CLOSING column is incorrect.
   C. Both totals are incorrect.
   D. Both totals are correct.

   1._____

2. For John Doe's tour of duty, the entries made in the DIFFERENCE column associated with the OPENING and CLOSING turnstile readings are shown as 1187, 162, 1546, and 63.
   Select the statement below which BEST describes the accuracy of these differences.

   A. 1187 is incorrect while 162, 1546 and 63 are correct.
   B. 1187 and 63 are incorrect while 1546 and 162 are correct.
   C. 63 is incorrect while 1187, 162 and 1546 are correct.
   D. 1187 and 1546 are incorrect while 162 and 63 are correct.

   2._____

3. For John Doe's tour of duty, select the statement below which BEST describes the accuracy of the amount $896.80 which he computed for NET FARES AT TOKEN VALUE. It

   A. is correct.
   B. should be $10.00 higher
   C. should be $100.00 higher
   D. should be $100.00 lower

   3._____

COMBINED RAILROAD CLERKS DAILY FARE REPORT

BEGINNING AT ☐ 10PM ☒ 11PM ☐ 12 M ☐ Other MONDAY DAY 1/6

ENDING AT ☐ 10PM ☒ 11PM ☐ 12 M ☐ Other TUES. DAY

	Column No. 1		Column No. 2

NAME (Print): JOHN DOE
Time from 11PM **to** 7AM
Pass # 17893W

NAME (Print): JOE SMITH
Time from 7AM **to** 3PM
Pass # 18495X

	Opening Reading at 10PM	Closing Reading at 6AM	Difference	Audit (Leave Blank)	Opening Reading at 6AM	Closing Reading at 2PM	Difference	Audit (Leave Blank)
1	85 123	86 210	1 187		86 210	87 489	1 279	
2	63 264	63 426	162		63 422	65 897	2 475	
3	20 126	21 672	1 546		21 672	22 908	1 236	
4	31 267	31 320	53		31 320	31 962	642	
5								
6								
7								
8								
9								
10								
T	199 780	202 628	2 848		202 624	207 256	5 632	

Add	Unregistered Fares (explain in remarks)			Add	Unregistered Fares (explain in remarks)		11
	TOTAL FARES	2848			TOTAL FARES		5632
Deduct	Slugs, mutilated foreign tokens registered in turnstiles	—		Deduct	Slugs, mutilated foreign tokens registered in turnstiles	23	
	Test Rings-Turnstile #	—			Test Rings-Turnstile #	6	
	NET FARES	2848			NET FARES		5603
1 NET FARES AT TOKEN VALUE		$896 80		1 NET FARES AT TOKEN VALUE			$1961 05
Token Reserve at Start		6100		Token Reserve at Start		5600	
Add Tokens Received		3000		Add Tokens Received		1400	
Deduct Tokens Transferred Out		3500		Deduct Tokens Transferred Out		2100	
TOTAL TOKEN RESERVE		5600		TOTAL TOKEN RESERVE		4900	
Deduct Token Reserve at End		5600		Deduct Token Reserve at End		3242	
2 Value of Reserve Tokens Sold		— —		2 Value of Reserve Tokens Sold		1758	$615 30
TOTAL ADD (LINES 1-2)		$896 80		TOTAL ADD (LINES 1-2)			$2576 35
Add Remittance for Prior Shortage				Add Remittance for Prior Shortage			
Deduct Deduction for Prior Overage		11 15		Deduct Deduction for Prior Overage			
NET AMOUNT DUE		$907 15		NET AMOUNT DUE			$2576 35

Rec'd. (Leave Blank)   Rec'd. (Leave Blank)

4. For John Doe's tour of duty, select the statement below which BEST describes the accuracy of the amount 5600
which he computed for TOTAL TOKEN RESERVE.
It

   A. is correct.
   B. should be 6500 higher.
   C. should be 500 higher.
   D. should be 3500 lower.

5. For Joe Smith's tour of duty, select the statement below which BEST describes the accuracy of the CLOSING total of 207256 computed by him.
It is

   A. correct.
   B. too high by 100.
   C. too low by 1000.
   D. too low by 10000.

6. For Joe Smith's tour of duty, select the statement below which BEST describes the accuracy of the NET FARES entry of 5603.
It is

   A. correct.
   B. too low by 11.
   C. too low by 29.
   D. too low by 36.

7. For Joe Smith's tour of duty, select the statement below which BEST describes the accuracy of the amount $615.30
which he computed for the VALUE OF RESERVE TOKENS SOLD.
It is

   A. correct.
   B. too low by $1.00.
   C. too high by $25.00
   D. too high by $35.00.

Questions 8-14.

DIRECTIONS: Questions 8 to 14 are based on the portion of a COMBINED RAILROAD CLERKS DAILY FARE REPORT shown on the next page. Some of the computed entries in this report may not be mathematically correct. In answering the questions, you are to determine the accuracy of certain computed entries. You are to assume that all entries which are not computed on this report but which are copies or transferred from another source, such as OPENING readings and TOKENS RECEIVED entries, are correct. NO OTHER ASSUMPTIONS ABOUT THE CORRECTNESS OF ENTRIES CAN BE MADE.

8. For Mary Spring's tour of duty, the entries made in the DIFFERENCE column associated with the OPENING and CLOSING turnstile readings are shown as 656, 1045, 1494, and 797. Select the statement below which BEST describes the accuracy of these differences computed by her.

   A. 1045 is incorrect while 656, 1494 and 797 are correct.
   B. 1494 is incorrect while 656, 1045 and 797 are correct.
   C. 797 is incorrect while 656, 1045 and 1494 are correct.
   D. 656, 1045, 1494 and 797 are all correct.

COMBINED RAILROAD CLERKS DAILY FARE REPORT

BEGINNING AT ☐ 10 PM / ☒ 11 PM _WEDNES._DAY _1/22_ / ☐ 12 M / ☐ Other

ENDING AT ☐ 10 PM / ☒ 11 PM _THURS._DAY / ☐ 12 M / ☐ Other

Column No. `1` Column No. `2`

	Column No. 1				Column No. 2			
NAME (Print)	_MARY SPRING_				_HELEN FALL_			
Time from	_11PM_ to _7AM_				_7AM_ to _3PM_			
	Pass # `30456Y`				Pass # `79846T`			
	Opening Reading at _10PM_	Closing Reading at _6AM_	Differ-ence	Audit (Leave Blank)	Opening Reading at _6AM_	Closing Reading at _2PM_	Differ-ence	Audit (Leave Blank)
1	34 767	35 423	656		35 423	36 411	988	
2	56 689	57 734	1 045		57 734	58 856	1 122	
3	76 474	77 968	1 494		77 968	78 649	681	
4	21 546	22 343	797		22 343	22 987	644	
5								
6								
7								
8								
9								
10								
T	189 466	193 468	3 992		193 368	196 803	3 435	
Add	Unregistered Fares (explain in remarks)			14	Unregistered Fares (explain in remarks)			17
	TOTAL FARES			3978	TOTAL FARES			3452
Deduct	Slugs, mutilated foreign tokens registered in turnstiles		17		Slugs, mutilated foreign tokens registered in turnstiles		14	
	Test Rings– Turnstile #		4		Test Rings– Turnstile #		3	
	NET FARES			3999	NET FARES			3435
1 NET FARES AT TOKEN VALUE				$1399 65	1 NET FARES AT TOKEN VALUE			$1202 25
Token Reserve at Start			6300		Token Reserve at Start		5800	
Add	Tokens Received		1200		Tokens Received		1400	
Deduct	Tokens Transferred Out		1700		Tokens Transferred Out		2700	
TOTAL TOKEN RESERVE			5800		TOTAL TOKEN RESERVE		4500	
Deduct	Token Reserve at End		5800		Token Reserve at End		1843	
2 Value of Reserve Tokens Sold			– –	– – –	2 Value of Reserve Tokens Sold		2657	$ 929 95
TOTAL ADD (LINES 1-2)				$1399 65	TOTAL ADD (LINES 1-2)			$2132 20
Add	Remittance for Prior Shortage				Remittance for Prior Shortage			4 30
Deduct	Deduction for Prior Overage				Deduction for Prior Overage			
	NET AMOUNT DUE			$1399 65	NET AMOUNT DUE			$2136 50

Rec'd. (Leave Blank)   Rec'd. (Leave Blank)

9. For Mary Spring's tour of duty, select the statement which ! BEST describes the accuracy of the OPENING total of 189466.
It is

   A. correct.
   B. too low by 10.
   C. too low by 100.
   D. too high by 100.

10. For Mary Spring's tour of duty, select the statement which BEST describes the accuracy of the NET FARES entry of 3999.
It is

   A. correct.
   B. too low by 28.
   C. too high by 42.
   D. too high by 14.

11. For Mary Spring's tour of duty, select the statement below which BEST describes the accuracy of the amount 5800 which she computed for TOTAL TOKEN RESERVE.
It is

   A. correct.
   B. too low by 3400.
   C. too low by 1000.
   D. too high by 2400.

12. For Helen Fall's tour of duty, the entries made on line *T* in the OPENING, CLOSING, and DIFFERENCE columns are 193368, 196803 and 3435, respectively.
Select the statement below which BEST describes the accuracy of these totals.

   A. 193368, 196803 and 3435 are *all* incorrect.
   B. 193368 is incorrect while 196803 and 3435 are correct.
   C. 193368 and 196803 are incorrect while 3435 is correct.
   D. 193368, 196803 and 3435 are *all* correct.

13. For Helen Fall's tour of duty, select the statement below which BEST describes the accuracy of the amount of $1202.25 which she computed for NET FARES AT TOKEN VALUE.
It

   A. is correct.
   B. should be $1.00 lower.
   C. should be $11.90 higher.
   D. should be $100.00 lower.

14. For Helen Fall's tour of duty, select the statement below which BEST describes the accuracy of the amount $929.95 which she computed for VALUE OF RESERVE TOKENS SOLD.
It

   A. is correct.
   B. should be $35.00 lower.
   C. should be $25.00 lower.
   D. should be $10.00 lower.

15. Assume that you, as an assistant station supervisor, are writing a report to your station supervisor in which you recommend changes in an existing standard operating procedure.
Of the following, the MOST important information that should be included in this report is a

A. list of basic reasons why the proposed altered procedure is better than the currently used one
B. timetable for putting the recommended changes into effect
C. complete detailed description of the present procedure
D. list of the names and titles of station department employees affected by the procedure changes

16. When you learn that an employee under your supervision is dissatisfied with his job, your FIRST action as an assistant station supervisor should be to

A. refer the matter to your station supervisor
B. try to find out the reason for his dissatisfaction
C. warn the employees not to spread his complaints to others
D. tell the employees that since others are not dissatisfied he should not be

Questions 17 - 21.

DIRECTIONS: Questions 17 to 21 require computing basic schedule working time for certain specified tasks for porters, You are to use the AVERAGE WORKING TIME FOR ONE PORTER, which is shown below, in computing the answers to these questions.

AVERAGE WORKING TIME FOR ONE PORTER

Task	Time
Sweeping Stairways	8 minutes per stairway
Scrapping Floor Areas	15,000 square feet per hour
Sweeping Floor Areas	5,500 square feet per hour
Cleaning Tile (7 to 9 ft. high)	50 linear feet per hour
Cleaning Tile (10 to 12 ft. high)	40 linear feet per hour
Cleaning Columns	6 per hour

17. A station has tile walls that are 7-1/2 ft. high.
The TOTAL computed time for cleaning 3,735 linear feet of the tile in this station once a month is, *most nearly*, _____ hours.

A. 7.5   B. 9.3   C. 74.7   D. 93.4

18. The TOTAL computed time for cleaning 126 columns in a station once a month over, a period of one year is_____ hours.

A. 21   B. 61   C. 252   D. 1512

19. The TOTAL weekly computed time for scrapping the floor area of a station having a northbound platform area of 14,640 square feet and a southbound platform area of 14,260 square feet three times a week is *closest to* _____ hours and _____ minutes.

A. 5; 47   B. 5; 17   C. 3; 10   D. 1; 55

20. The TOTAL weekly computed time for sweeping seven stairways twice a week at a station is

A. 56 minutes
B. 1 hour and 52 minutes
C. 2 hours and 2 minutes
D. 2 hours and 12 minutes

21. The TOTAL weekly computed time for sweeping both the northbound and southbound platforms of a station, where each has a floor area of 13,670 square feet, twice a week, is *closest to* _____ hours. 21._____

    A. 4.9 B. 8.8 C. 9.9 D. 19.9

22. One of the railroad clerks in a booth sees a passenger, who appears to be intoxicated and unable to take care of himself, outside the booth stumbling towards a turnstile. Following are four possible courses of action which this railroad clerk could take which might be correct: 22._____
    I. Have the passenger placed in the charge of a transit patrolman
    II. Have the passenger placed in the charge of an assistant station supervisor
    III. Allow the passenger to pay his fare and enter through the turnstile if there is a transit patrolman present
    IV. Allow the passenger to pay his fare and enter through the turnstile, but don't allow him to go onto the platform without assistance

    Which of the following choices lists ALL of the above courses of action that are *correct* and lists NONE that is *incorrect*?

    A. I and II   B. I, II, and III
    C. I and III   D. II and IV

23. With the exception of those keys under the jurisdiction of the transportation department, the keys to the emergency rooms at the end of each rapid transit river tunnel are kept 23._____

    A. at designated booths at either end of the tunnels
    B. at the nearest field office
    C. by assistant station supervisors
    D. in special lockers outside these rooms

24. Part of a rule for station supervisors states as follows: 24._____
    He will keep a running inventory showing the supplies received and the distribution made by date and by station.
    Of the following, the idea which is CLOSEST to the basic meaning of the above instruction is that assistant station supervisors must

    A. keep a continuous record of supplies received and distributed
    B. keep an accurate record of the cost of supplies received and distributed
    C. periodically update their summary inventories
    D. maintain a fast moving inventory

25. When a supervisor gives instructions to a subordinate employee about a specific task, the amount of detailed information that the supervisor should give him depends PRIMARILY on 25._____

    A. the difficulty of the job and how long the job will take
    B. the difficulty of the job and the amount of experience the employee has
    C. how long the job will take and the amount of experience the employee has
    D. how long the job will take and how much time the subordinate has to listen

KEY (CORRECT ANSWERS)

1. D
2. B
3. C
4. A
5. C

6. B
7. D
8. D
9. B
10. D

11. A
12. C
13. A
14. B
15. A

16. B
17. C
18. C
19. A
20. B

21. C
22. A
23. A
24. A
25. B

TEST 2

DIRECTIONS: Each question or incomplete statement is followed by several suggested answers or completions. Select the one that BEST answers the question or completes the statement. *PRINT THE LETTER OF THE CORRECT ANSWER IN THE SPACE AT THE RIGHT.*

1. When an employee has discovered a fire on transit authority property and has used a fire extinguisher to put out the fire, he should return the extinguisher to the exact location from which it was taken, PRIMARILY so that

   A. it will not be reported missing
   B. it will be ready for immediate reuse in case of another fire
   C. it is placed out of the way and will not be a tripping hazard
   D. no delay will occur in having it refilled

1.____

Questions 2-5.

DIRECTIONS: Questions 2 to 6 are based on the paragraphs shown below entitled, *Posting of Diversion of Service Notices*. Refer to these paragraphs when answering these questions.

POSTING OF DIVERSION OF SERVICE NOTICES

The following procedures concerning the receiving and posting of service diversion notices will be strictly adhered to:

Station supervisors who receive notices will sign a receipt and return it to the Station Department office. It will be their responsibility to ensure that all notices are posted at affected stations and a notation made in the transmittal logs. All excess notices will be tied and a notation made thereon, indicating the stations and the date notices were posted, and the name and pass number of the assistant station supervisor posting same. The word *Excess* is to be boldly written on bundled notices and the bundle placed in a conspicuous location. When loose notices, without any notations, are discovered in any field office, assistant station supervisor's office or other Station Department locations, the matter is to be thoroughly investigated to make sure proper distribution has been completed. All stations where a diversion of service exists must be contacted daily by the assistant station supervisor covering that group and hour to ensure that a sufficient number of notices are posted and employees are aware of the situation. In any of the above circumstances, notation is to be made in the supervisory log. Station supervisors will be responsible for making certain all affected stations in their respective groups have notices posted and for making spot checks each day diversions are in effect.

2. A station supervisor who has signed a receipt upon receiving service diversion notices must return the

   A. notice to the Station Department office
   B. receipt to the Station Department office
   C. receipt and the transmittal log to the affected stations
   D. transmittal log after making a notation in it

2.____

23

3. Of the following, the information which is NOT required to be written on a bundle of excess notices is the

   A. names of the stations where the notices were posted
   B. time of day when the notices were posted
   C. date when the notices were posted
   D. name and pass number of the assistant station supervisor posting the notices

4. If loose notices without notations on them are found, the situation should be investigated to make sure that the

   A. notices are properly returned to the Station Department
   B. assistant station supervisor responsible for the error is found
   C. notices are correct for the diversion involved
   D. notices have been distributed properly

5. To insure that employees are aware of a diversion in service, an assistant station supervisor covering the group and hour when a diversion exists must contact the involved stations

   A. immediately after the diversion
   B. on an hourly basis
   C. on a daily basis
   D. as often as possible

6. To make certain affected stations have notices posted when diversions occur, *spot cheoks* should be made by

   A. station supervisors daily
   B. station supervisors when necessary
   C. assistant station supervisors daily
   D. assistant station supervisors when necessay

7. An employee who has been absent due to illness must submit a sick leave application within _____ after his return to work.

   A. two days
   B. three days
   C. five days
   D. one week

8. Except at heavily traveled areas, the rear section of all trains will be closed off and isolated between the hours of_____ daily.

   A. 7 p.m. and 5 p.m.
   B. 8 p.m. and 4 a.m.
   C. 9 p.m. and 6 a.m.
   D. 10 p.m. and 5 a.m.

9. A passenger notices that you, a station supervisor, have come out of a booth and he angrily complains to you about poor subway conditions.
   Of the following, the BEST procedure for you to follow in this case is to

   A. listen to him courteously and avoid, if possible, making any argumentative statements
   B. tell the passenger to complain to the mayor's office
   C. tell the passenger that nothing can be done about the situation because of current budgetary problems
   D. indicate to the passenger that you agree with him

10. If a supervisor finds it necessary for the first time to criticize a subordinate for poor work performance, it is MOST important that he should

    A. make sure that the subordinate is in a good mood before criticizing him
    B. make sure others are present in order to set an example for them also
    C. be specific in his criticism to the subordinate
    D. criticize the subordinate harshly to make sure his performance improves

11. According to the station department manual of instructions, the major duties performed by a porter at a station are defined as those duties that

    A. are more important than others
    B. involve greater physical effort to perform
    C. are performed daily
    D. are performed on certain days of the week

12. The transit authority rules state that an employee must undergo a medical examination by the transit authority medical staff before being permitted to return to work if he has been absent on sick leave *more than* _____ consecutive calendar days.

    A. 14   B. 21   C. 28   D. 35

Questions 13-18.

DIRECTIONS: Questions 13 to 18 are based on the chart of HOURLY TURNSTILE READINGS shown below. Refer to this chart when answering these questions.

HOURLY TURNSTILE READINGS

Turnstile No.	2 P.M.	3 P.M.	4 P.M.	5 P.M.	6 P.M.
1	79062	81134	81968	82450	83639
2	38829	39663	40243	42598	44333
3	14376	14693	14898	14987	15036
4	55444	55582	55647	55839	55989

13. The turnstile which registered the LARGEST number of fares between 3 P.M. and 5 P.M. is

    A. No. 1   B. No. 2   C. No. 3   D. No. 4

14. The turnstile which registered the LOWEST number of fares between 2 P.M. and 3 P.M. is

    A. No. 1   B. No. 2   C. No. 3   D. No. 4

15. The *total number* of passengers using Turnstile No. 2 from 2 P.M. to 6 P.M. is

    A. 5504   B. 5505   C. 5515   D. 5604

16. The *total number* of passengers using all four turnstiles from 3 P.M. to 4 P.M. is

    A. 1574   B. 1674   C. 1684   D. 1784

17. Turnstile No. 1 registered the LOWEST number of passengers between _____ P.M. and _____ .M.

    A. 2; 3   B. 3; 4   C. 4; 5   D. 5; 6

18. Turnstile No. 3 registered the HIGHEST number of passengers between _____ P.M. and _____ P.M.

    A. 2; 3   B. 3; 4   C. 4; 5   D. 5; 6

19. According to the rules and regulations, a railroad clerk who calls in sick must do so *at least* _____ hour(s) before the start of his tour of duty.

    A. 1/2   B. 1   C. 2   D. 3

20. The location of an emergency alarm box for removing third rail power is indicated by _____ light(s).

    A. a red
    B. three amber
    C. a lunar white
    D. a blue

21. The information contained in station department bulletin orders covers PRIMARILY

    A. revisions in the station department manual of instructions
    B. matters of ordinary routine for all employees
    C. instructions for non-supervisory employees
    D. matters of an operational nature which are usually permanent

22. The train horn signal consisting of a series of long-short-long-short blasts means that the train

    A. crew needs assistance
    B. needs a road car inspector
    C. is passing caution lights or flags and is warning a flagman of its approach
    D. has run past or stopped short of the station platform

23. Of the following, the BEST course of action for a station supervisor to follow when he observes a porter for the first time scrapping a platform in an unsatisfactory way is to

    A. reprimand the porter and tell him to do better the next time
    B. make several more checks on the porter to determine whether he does his other tasks satisfactorily
    C. discuss the situation with his station supervisor
    D. demonstrate to the porter the proper way of doing the work and then observe him doing it

24. In case a station supervisor sees smoke in the subway, he should *immediately* call the

    A. fire department
    B. desk trainmaster
    C. transit police
    D. maintenance of way department

25. If a porter observes an unauthorized vendor selling his goods in a station, the porter should *immediately* report this to 25.____

    A. the police
    B. his assistant station supervisor
    C. the office of the assistant general superintendent, stations
    D. the transit police

KEY (CORRECT ANSWERS)

1. D
2. B
3. B
4. D
5. C

6. A
7. B
8. B
9. A
10. C

11. D
12. B
13. B
14. D
15. A

16. C
17. C
18. A
19. B
20. D

21. D
22. A
23. D
24. B
25. D

TEST 3

DIRECTIONS: Each question or incomplete statement is followed by several suggested answers or completions. Select the one that BEST answers the question or completes the, statement. *PRINT THE LETTER OF THE CORREC ANSWER IN THE SPACE AT THE RIGHT.*

1. Each employee who receives lost property will be held responsible for it

    A. and will be able to claim it as his own after three months
    B. unless he can produce a receipt for it from another employee
    C. until it is claimed by its owner
    D. until the time it reaches the Lost Property Office

    1._____

2. The *total number* of zones that the station department operates is

    A. 4   B. 6   C. 8   D. 10

    2._____

3. At 11:00 A.M., on a Tuesday, a porter reports to his station supervisor that a heavy piece of equipment fell on him and injured his foot.
Unless the employee needs immediate hospital attention, the PROPER course of action for the assistant station supervisor to take is to

    A. have the porter make out an accident report and send him to a transit authority clinic
    B. fill out an accident report and tell the porter to continue his normal duties
    C. tell the porter to sign out and see his family doctor if necessary
    D. tell the porter to go back to his job and wait for a replacement before going home

    3._____

4. In an emergency, when it is necessary to remove power from the third rail and there is no emergency alarm box available, power may be removed by telephoning the

    A. station department office, control desk
    B. power distribution division
    C. nearest train dispatcher
    D. desk trainmaster of the division involved

    4._____

5. When a low turnstile at a station becomes inoperative, the railroad clerk on duty must *immediately* notify

    A. his assistant station supervisor
    B. the station department office, control desk
    C. the turnstile subdivision, maintenance of way department
    D. the appropriate field office

    5._____

6. The train horn signal consisting of two long blasts means that the train

    A. crew needs assistance
    B. needs a signal maintainer
    C. is passing caution lights or flags and is warning a flagman of its approach
    D. is passing through the station without stopping

    6._____

7. A person has been injured by tripping and falling down the stairs in a station and has been given assistance by a railroad clerk. The railroad clerk finds it necessary to turn over the injured person to the care of another transit authority employee.
   For the purpose of filling out the necessary reports, both employees must exchange names,_____ .

   A. and pass numbers only
   B. titles, and pass numbers
   C. and titles only
   D. titles, and assigned work locations

7._____

8. A booth in a station that is manned continuously and where the railroad clerk is in general charge of the station is classified as a(n)_____ booth.

   A. station head   B. area control
   C. transfer   D. 24-hour

8._____

9. The transfer of change funds from one station booth to another

   A. is never permitted
   B. is permitted without any special authorization
   C. can be made between part-time booths and control booths
   D. is permitted in emergencies if authorized by a railroad clerk in general charge of a station

9._____

Questions 10-14.

DIRECTIONS: Questions 10 to 14 are based on the paragraphs shown below covering the supply duties of assistant station supervisors. Refer to these paragraphs when answering these questions.

SUPPLY DUTIES OF ASSISTANT STATION SUPERVISORS

The assistant station supervisors on the 8 a.m. to 4 p.m. tour will be responsible for the ordering of porter cleaning supplies and will inventory individual stations under their jurisdiction in order to maintain the necessary supplies to insure proper sanitary standards. They will be responsible not only for the ordering of such supplies but will see to it that ordered supplies are distributed as required in accordance with order supply sheets. Assistant station supervisors on the 4 p.m. to 12 midnight and 12 midnight to 8 a.m. shift will cooperate with the a.m. station supervisor to properly control supplies.

The 4 p.m. to 12 midnight assistant station supervisors will be responsible for the ordering and control of all stationery supplies used by railroad clerks in the performance of their duties. They will also see that supplies are kept in a neat and orderly manner,. The assistant station supervisors in charge of *Supply Storerooms* will see to it that material so ordered will be given to the porters for delivery to the respective booths. Cooperation of all supervision applies in this instance.

The 12 midnight to 8 a.m. assistant station supervisors will be responsible for the storing of materials delivered by special work train (sawdust, etc.). They will also see that all revenue bags which are torn, dirty, etc., are picked up and sent to the field office for delivery to the bag room.

Any supplies needed other than those distributed on regular supply days will be requested by submitting a requisition to the supply control desk for emergency delivery.

10. The assistant station supervisors who are responsible for ordering all stationery supplies used by railroad clerks are the ones on the _____ tour.

    A. 8 a.m. to 4 p.m.
    B. 4 p.m. to 12 midnight
    C. 12 midnight to 8 a.m.
    D. 4 p.m. to 2 p.m.

11. Storing of materials delivered by special work trains is the responsibility of assistant station supervisors on the _____ tour.

    A. 8 a.m. to 4 p.m.
    B. 4 p.m. to 12 midnight
    C. 12 midnight to 8 a.m.
    D. 4 p.m. to 2 p.m.

12. Torn revenue bags should be picked up and sent FIRST to

    A. the bag room
    B. the supply control desk
    C. a supply storeroom
    D. the field office

13. To obtain an emergency delivery of supplies on a day other than a regular supply day, a requisition should be submitted to the

    A. appropriate zone office
    B. appropriate field office
    C. supply control desk
    D. station supervisor

14. The assistant station supervisor responsible for ordering porter cleaning supplies will inventory individual stations PRIMARILY for the end purpose of

    A. insuring proper sanitary standards
    B. maintaining necessary supplies
    C. keeping track of supplies
    D. distributing supplies fairly

15. A collecting agent may reveal a combination to a safe if he

    A. has a written order from the superintendent of stations
    B. is verbally instructed to do so by the station supervisor
    C. reports this action in writing to the station department assistant general superintendent
    D. has the written permission of the assistant station supervisor to whom he reports

16. The train starting signal at terminal stations and the train holding signal at gap stations consist of *three* _____ lights.

    A. blue
    B. lunar white
    C. red
    D. amber

17. According to the rules and regulations, assistant station supervisors have certain duties 17.____
and responsibilities. Following are four duties and responsibilities of assistant station
supervisors which might be correct:
   I. They report to station supervisors and to other superior officers of the station
      department and the rapid transit operations department.
   II. They are in charge of designated groups of stations or other designated
       areas.
   III. They determine that current work schedules for employees under their juris-
        diction provide efficient and effective service.
   IV. They supervise the installation of turnstiles in stations.
Which of the following choices lists ALL of the above duties and responsibilities that
are correct and lists NONE that is incorrect?

   A. I, II, and III   B. I, II, III, and IV
   C. II and III   D. II, III, and IV

18. After a robbery has taken place at a booth, the railroad clerk involved must take certain 18.____
immediate steps. Following are four *immediate* steps that might be correct:
   I. Notify the police using the appropriate telephone extension
   II. Notify the station department office and the field office
   III. Check the booth accounts and ascertain the loss
   IV. Submit a complete written report of the occurrence
Which of the fdllqwing choices lists ALL of the above steps that are correct and lists
NO steps that is *incorrect?*

   A. I, II, III, and IV   B. I, II, and IV
   C. I, III, and IV   D. II, III, and IV

19. When giving instructions to a porter, you will *most likely* avoid confusing him if you (your) 19.____

   A. instructions are as detailed as possible
   B. instructions are clear and concise
   C. repeat your instructions to him several times using different words each time
   D. give him the instructions as quickly as possible

20. A supervisor who is performing his job well should be checking all operations under his 20.____
jurisdiction.
Of the following, the LEAST important reason for doing this is to make certain that

   A. he personally observes all operations as they are performed
   B. all the operations are still needed
   C. subordinates are performing their work efficiently
   D. operations are being performed as scheduled

21. The train that goes to Far Rockaway is the _____ train. 21.____

   A. A   B. E
   C. F   D. number 2

22. In order to travel by subway to Ditmars Boulevard and 31 Street in Astoria, it is necessary 22.____
to take the_____ train.

   A. N   B. B
   C. number 7   D. F

23. The number *1* train travels between   23._____

    A. Pelham Bay Park and Brooklyn Bridge at Worth Street
    B. Van Cortlandt Park and South Ferry
    C. Woodlawn and Utica Avenue
    D. Dyre Avenue and Atlantic Avenue

24. When preparing a report about an unusual occurrence it is LEAST important to   24._____

    A. be accurate on the details
    B. make the report lengthy in description
    C. be clear in describing the incident
    D. leave out unimportant details

25. The transit authority sick leave *year* is defined as the period between   25._____

    A. January 1 and December 31
    B. April 1 and March 31
    C. May 1 and April 30
    D. July 1 and June 30

26. If a station supervisor suspects that a porter is unfit for duty because of alcohol, he should   26._____

    A. ask the porter whether he can perform his work
    B. direct the porter to submit to a blood-alcohol examination
    C. suspend the porter and discipline him
    D. tell the porter to return to work when he sobers up

27. According to the station department manual of instructions, a station department employee may exchange a tour of duty with another employee *provided* he has received specific permission from   27._____

    A. his immediate supervisor
    B. his field office
    C. the station department office
    D. the assistant general superintendent stations

28. A passenger tells a station department employee that he fell on a station platform and he wants to know how to file a claim against the transit authority.
    The PROPER procedure for the employee to follow is to tell the passenger   28._____

    A. that he cannot give him any information
    B. that he will file an accident report and a claim for damages for the passenger
    C. to leave his name and address and that a member of the transit authority managerial staff will contact him
    D. to contact the transit authority's law department at Jay Street

29. According to step 1 of the grievance procedure, a railroad clerk may present a grievance to his assistant station supervisor   29._____

- A. orally or through his union only
- B. orally or in writing personally only
- C. orally, or in writing personally, or through his union
- D. in writing personally or through his union only

30. After an aggrieved railroad clerk has received a step 1 decision, he may appeal this decision within   30._____

   A. 48 hours   B. 3 days   C. 5 days   D. 1 week

KEY (CORRECT ANSWERS)

1.	B	16.	D
2.	C	17.	C
3.	A	18.	D
4.	D	19.	B
5.	B	20.	A
6.	C	21.	A
7.	B	22.	A
8.	A	23.	B
9.	C	24.	B
10.	B	25.	C
11.	C	26.	B
12.	D	27.	C
13.	C	28.	D
14.	A	29.	C
15.	A	30.	B

EXAMINATION SECTION
TEST 1

DIRECTIONS: Each question or incomplete statement is followed by several suggested answers for completions. Select the one that BEST answers the question or completes the statement. *PRINT THE LETTER OF THE CORRECT ANSWER IN THE SPACE AT THE RIGHT.*

1. Good supervision requires that the station supervisor visit his assigned stations

    A. on a fixed schedule only
    B. as many times a day as possible
    C. only when trouble develops
    D. at random as well as regular intervals

2. At a subway station located in the financial district, a station supervisor would normally expect the GREATEST concentration of passenger traffic to occur from

    A. 6:30 A.M. to 8:00 A.M.
    B. 7:30 A.M. to 8:30 A.M.
    C. 4:00 P.M. to 5:30 P.M.
    D. 5:30 P.M. to 7:30 P.M.

3. The LEAST important reason for the requirement that all accidents on the transit system must be promptly investigated is that such investigation help to

    A. settle claims promptly
    B. fix responsibility
    C. set up a regular routine
    D. prevent similar accidents in the future

4. Two porters are to be assigned to a special cleaning job at a remote location. By placing the one with the better record in charge, the assistant supervisor will

    A. be showing good judgment
    B. know that the job will require no supervision on his part
    C. be following standard policy
    D. not be criticized if the job is poorly done

5. The BEST assurance a station supervisor can have that a railroad clerk knows how to do his work is if the clerk

    A. makes few mistakes
    B. is cooperative
    C. works quickly
    D. asks no questions

6. An accident involving an employee occurred on a job to which you had assigned two men.
   In questioning them separately to fix responsibility, you should be MAINLY interested in obtaining information pertaining to

    A. the ability and experience of each
    B. how well the other understood your instructions
    C. the manner in which the other performs his work
    D. what each was doing at the time the accident occurred

7. For the sake of safety while working under conditions which involve an element of danger, safety rules have been compiled

   A. to eliminate accidents
   B. to minimize time lost
   C. for the guidance of employees
   D. for avoiding dangerous assignments

8. Six porters can clean a certain tile wall in 3 hours. If two of the porters left one hour after starting work, the job would require _____ hours.

   A. 3 1/2   B. 4   C. 5   D. 9

9. Of the following the LEAST important element in good subway service is the

   A. size of the cars
   B. relative infrequency of breakdowns
   C. cleanliness of cars and stations
   D. courtesy of the employees

10. A report of an unusual occurrence is MOST likely to be accurate as to facts if written by the station supervisor

    A. before discussing matters with anyone
    B. right after the occurrence
    C. after discussion with the station supervisor
    D. the following day after thinking things over

11. The station supervisors on the 4 P.M. to midnight trick are responsible for the

    A. ordering and distribution of porter cleaning supplies
    B. storing of all special work train deliveries such as sawdust
    C. ordering and control of all stationery supplies used by railroad clerks
    D. for the collection of all torn and dirty revenue bags

12. If a porter reporting for duty falls and apparently sustains a broken leg, the station supervisor should immediately telephone the

    A. nearest T.A. clinic   B. first aid room
    C. supervisor's office   D. transit police

Questions 13-19.

DIRECTIONS: Questions 13 through 19 are based on the description of a special event given below. Refer to this description in answering these questions.

A special parade, on Thanksgiving Day, is to follow, for the first time, a line of march paralleling a nearby 4-track rapid transit line, and approximately 1 1/2 million spectators are anticipated. The parade is expected to take 3 hours to pass any given point and it will take 2 hours for any part of the parade to march from the beginning to the end of the route, starting near the Cliff Street express station at 10:00 A.M., marching north, and finishing near the Bank Street express station. There are 5 local stops between these points. No other rapid transit line is near the route of the parade although several surface lines cross the line of march. One terminal of the rapid transit line is about 30 minutes riding time from Cliff station via express, the other terminal is about 35 minutes riding time from Bank station via express, and the scheduled riding time from Cliff station to Bank station is 10 minutes via local and 6 minutes via express.

13. From the description of the event it is clear that one who wished to go from the Bank Street station to the Cliff Street station would have to travel

    A. north   B. south   C. east   D. west

14. The employees of this rapid transit line should expect a large number of passengers to enter at Cliff Street station starting at about

    A. 11:00 A.M.   B. 12:00 Noon   C. 1:00 P.M.   D. 3:00 P.M.

15. The employees of this rapid transit line should expect a large number of passengers to enter at Bank Street station starting at about

    A. 12:00 Noon   B. 1:00 P.M.
    C. 2:00 P.M.   D. 3:00 P.M.

16. The BEST place to make the count of passengers who come to watch the parade would be at

    A. the express stations   B. the local stations
    C. Bank Street   D. Cliff Street

17. If the local stops are uniformly spaced, the time it takes for any one part of the parade to march from one local station to the next is APPROXIMATELY _____ minutes.

    A. 10   B. 15   C. 20   D. 30

18. The riding time between the terminals of this line, via express, is

    A. 35 minutes   B. 1 hour and 5 minutes
    C. 1 hour and 11 minutes   D. 1 hour and 15 minutes

19. The BEST way to make the count of passengers who will probably use any particular station when the parade is over would be to

    A. assign personnel to all exits to count crowd leaving station
    B. count the number of tokens sold there to parade time
    C. take a turnstile count at that station until 12:00 P.M.
    D. estimate number of passengers exiting from trains stopping at that station

20. Ten car trains arrive on five minute intervals at a terminal station. Assuming that each car carries 120 passengers, the number of passengers exiting from the station in an hour is NEAREST to

    A. 8200   B. 12000   C. 14400   D. 16000

21. Of the following, the BEST way to have transit employees as a whole learn good safety habits is to

    A. penalize them with loss of pay for lost-time accidents
    B. let them learn through their own mistakes
    C. have them re-read the rules in their spare time
    D. offer prizes for the best safety records

22. To keep errors in station entrance computations to a minimum, turnstile meters

   A. are placed on each turnstile
   B. must be read at definite times
   C. require much maintenance
   D. have large and clear numbers

23. One of the duties of station supervisors is to

   A. immediately report infractions of the rules which come to their attention
   B. check daily to see that railroad clerks and porters have ample supplies
   C. be responsible for any tools or equipment left by the turnstile section on any of the stations in his area
   D. make any changes in Station Department Instructions that are necessary

24. A cleaner complains to you that the porter he relieves does not complete his share of the work and that he has been informed that this is due to frequent and lengthy conversations with passengers.
   The LEAST likely conclusion would be that the cleaner complained of

   A. is well liked by the regular passengers at that station
   B. lives near the station
   C. is a responsible individual
   D. has had words with the cleaner turning him in

25. You have noticed that one of the cleaners at a station in your area is frequently in the tower at the end of the platform. He tells you that he is studying for the next railroad clerk promotion examination whenever he gets a chance.
   As station supervisor you should

   A. overlook this situation since it is temporary and reasonable
   B. inform him that he is never permitted in the tower
   C. transfer the man to a station in the area without a tower
   D. insist that he discontinue this practice during working hours

26. A recently appointed cleaner is assigned to duty under your supervision.
   Of the following, the MOST important thing to do is

   A. make sure he knows all the rules and regulations in detail
   B. acquaint him with traffic conditions at his station
   C. familiarize him with the schedule of working conditions for station employees
   D. take him on a tour of the station to which he will be assigned pointing out his duties

27. A systematic layout of work and proper assignment of men to a special job, by a supervisor, will NOT affect the

   A. amount of work to be done
   B. quality of the finished work
   C. time required to do the work
   D. kind of supervision needed in the performance of the work

28. A station supervisor, telephoning from an agent's booth located on a subway platform, hears a train whistle signal that sounds to him like *short-long-short*.
    If the signal is not repeated and the railroad clerk also is not sure of what he heard, the assistant station supervisor could logically conclude that he had heard part of a signal and that the motorman was actually signaling to alert

    A. people standing too close to the edge of the platform to move back
    B. station or police personnel that assistance is needed
    C. his conductor that the train will overrun or stop short of the station marker
    D. a car inspector to meet the train as something needs correction

29. A station having a total platform area of 22,575 sq. ft. is to be swept twice a week.
    If the average area that can be swept per hour is 5,250 sq. ft., the total time to be allotted for the twice-weekly sweeping is CLOSEST to _____ hours, _____ minutes.

    A. 4; 6　　　B. 4; 18　　　C. 8; 36　　　D. 9; 20

30. For three adjacent stations for the same period, the first requires twice as much sawdust as the second and the second twice as much as the third.
    If 14 bags of sawdust are to be properly distributed to these stations, the first station should receive _____ bags.

    A. 4　　　B. 6　　　C. 8　　　D. 10

KEY (CORRECT ANSWERS)

1.	D	16.	A
2.	C	17.	C
3.	C	18.	C
4.	A	19.	A
5.	A	20.	C
6.	D	21.	D
7.	C	22.	B
8.	B	23.	A
9.	A	24.	C
10.	B	25.	D
11.	C	26.	D
12.	D	27.	A
13.	B	28.	B
14.	C	29.	C
15.	D	30.	C

TEST 2

DIRECTIONS: Each question or incomplete statement is followed by several suggested answers or completions. Select the one that BEST answers the question or completes the statement. *PRINT THE LETTER OF THE CORRECT ANSWER IN THE SPACE AT THE RIGHT.*

1. The official published Rules and Regulations are LEAST useful in   1.___

   A. helping employees in the proper performance of their duties
   B. relieving supervisory employees of their responsibility
   C. providing a fair basis for any necessary disciplinary action
   D. encouraging safe practices

2. An employee of the transit system should give his name and badge number at the request of any passenger   2.___

   A. without argument after first trying to placate the passenger
   B. without delay or argument
   C. if a valid reason is given
   D. if the passenger insists strenuously

3. It is particularly important that assistant station supervisors be acquainted with the various rapid transit and surface lines in order to   3.___

   A. be able to move quickly to another point when necessary
   B. make the best disposition of passengers in case of blockade
   C. be able to make recommendations for better service
   D. generally answer passenger questions in this regard

4. Considerable time of supervision is required in investigating complaints by passengers against employees.   4.___
   The BEST overall solution to this problem is to

   A. have supervisors stress courtesy in public relations
   B. set up a central complaint bureau
   C. send a standard courteous answer and omit investigation
   D. investigate only the legitimate complaints

5. It would be POOR supervision on the part of a station supervisor if he   5.___

   A. consulted an experienced railroad clerk on an unusual problem
   B. made it a policy to avoid criticizing a man while another was present
   C. overlooked minor infractions of the rules on occasions
   D. allowed several days to elapse before giving one of his men a deserved reprimand

Questions 6-11.

DIRECTIONS: Questions 6 through 11 are based on the tabulation of Turnstile Readings shown below. Consult this tabulation in answering these questions. Note that booth No. 74 is open 24 hours a day, the clerk on the midnight tour reporting at 11:00 P.M.

TURNSTILE READING

BOOTH NO. 74 - WEST STREET STATION

Sunday - August 5.

HOUR	TURNSTILE NUMBER				
	1	2	3	4	5
5 AM	72583	00602	08390	22924	98832
6 AM	72650	00631	08437	22983	98893
7 AM	72705	00648	08472	23031	98945
8 AM	72747	00659	08501	23067	98958
9 AM	72779	00666	08524	23094	99025
10 AM	72805	00675	08535	23127	99064
11 AM	72853	00693	08544	23159	99129
12 NOON	72947	00718	08621	23240	99200
1 PM	73124	00796	08794	23394	99348
2 PM	73430	00958	09039	23660	99625
3 PM	74005	01366	09572	24161	00169
4 PM	74925	02032	10309	24961	00905
5 PM	76002	02906	11261	25898	01876
6 PM	77202	03873	12360	27010	03018
7 PM	78385	04953	13470	28128	04155
8 PM	79500	05847	14467	29137	05172
9 PM	80571	06705	15459	30126	06177

6. From the information given it is MOST probable that the   6.____

   A. most used stairway from the street is nearest turnstile #4
   B. #3 turnstile has just recently been put back in service
   C. entrance stairways are farthest from turnstiles #2, #3, and #4
   D. change booth is nearest turnstile #5

7. One of the listed turnstile readings which should be unlikely to appear on the regular Combined Railroad Clerks Daily Fare Report is   7.____

   A. 00602   B. 08437   C. 73430   D. 99625

8. If turnstile Nos. 3 and 4 had been closed during the entire period of the above tabulation while the total passenger traffic remained the same, and the passengers that would have used turnstiles Nos. 3 and 4 were divided equally among the other three turnstiles, the reading of turnstile #2 at 9 P.M. would have been   8.____

   A. 8390   B. 10860   C. 11462   D. 14271

9. If 40% of the passengers entering through these turnstiles on August 5th were registered in the six hours from 3 P.M. to 9 P.M., the total number of passengers registered this day was APPROXIMATELY

   A. 74500 B. 76000 C. 78000 D. 79500

10. The average number of passengers per minute using turnstile #2 during the busiest hour was NEAREST to

    A. 17 B. 18 C. 19 D. 20

11. The total number of passengers using turnstile #2 during the period from 5 P.M. to 8 P.M. was NEAREST to the number of passengers using turnstile

    A. #4 from 1 P.M. to 5 P.M.
    B. #3 from 8 A.M. to 5 P.M.
    C. #1 from 4 P.M. to 7 P.M.
    D. #5 from 4 P.M. to 7 P.M.

Questions 12-14.

DIRECTIONS: Questions 12 through 14 are based on the situation described below. Consider the facts given in this situation when answering these questions.

SITUATION

A new detergent that is to be added to water and the resulting mixture just wiped on any surface has been tested by the station department and appeared to be excellent. However you notice, after inspecting a large number of stations that your porters have cleaned with this detergent, that the surfaces cleaned are not as clean as they formerly were when the old method was used.

12. The MAIN reason for the station department testing the new detergent in the first place was to make certain that

    A. it was very simple to use
    B. a little bit would go a long way
    C. there was no stronger detergent on the market
    D. it was superior to anything formerly used

13. The MAIN reason that such a poor cleaning job resulted was MOST likely due to the

    A. porters being lax on the job
    B. detergent not being as good as expected
    C. incorrect amount of water being mixed with the detergent
    D. fact that the surfaces cleaned needed to be scrubbed

14. The reason for inspecting a number of stations was to

    A. determine whether all porters did the same job
    B. insure that the result of the cleaning job was the same in each location
    C. be certain that the detergent was used in each station inspected
    D. see whether certain surfaces cleaned better than others

15. A passenger asks you, the station supervisor, for directions on how to get to a certain 15.____
    place on the transit system.
    If you do not know the answer you should tell the passenger

    A. that you do not know and try to direct him to someone who does know
    B. to look the answer up on the subway map posted at the station
    C. that only railroad clerks are able to give such directions
    D. to get aboard the next train and to ask the conductor

16. The Employee Suggestion Plan is beneficial to transit authority employees because they 16.____

    A. become more efficient employees after making a suggestion
    B. are certain to be rewarded for making suggestions
    C. have an opportunity to express their ideas with management
    D. acquaint themselves with the ideas of fellow employees

17. The LEAST valuable source of information for improvements in bagging procedures is 17.____

    A. suggestions of employees
    B. recommendations from the auditing department
    C. assistant supervisor's records
    D. the Authority's Rules and Regulations

18. A railroad clerk working 12:00 midnight to 8:00 A.M. is directed to report to the NYCTA 18.____
    medical staff for a physical examination at 11:00 A.M. of the same day. The pay allowed
    him for reporting will be _____ hour(s).

    A. 1   B. 2   C. 3   D. 4

Questions 19-22.

DIRECTIONS: Questions 19 through 22 are based on the situation described below. Consider
             the facts given in this situation when answering these questions.

SITUATION

John Doe desiring to get to the Stillwell Avenue Station in Coney Island boarded a Manhattan bound train at the Continental Avenue Station in Forest Hills at 11:30 A.M. on a weekday.

19. The total number of lines going to Manhattan from Continental Avenue at this time of day 19.____
    is

    A. 2   B. 3   C. 4   D. 5

20. A good transfer point where Doe may change trains to reach his destination is 20.____

    A. 59th Street and Lexington Avenue
    B. 34th Street and 6th Avenue
    C. 42nd Street and 8th Avenue
    D. Queens Plaza

21. The train which Doe should board to make the trip in the SHORTEST possible time started from

    A. Continental Avenue
    B. 179th Street
    C. 169th Street
    D. Parsons Blvd.

22. A train he could have transferred to in order to reach his destination without additional change is

    A. IND "A" train
    B. BMT Brighton Express
    C. BMT West End Express
    D. IND "D" train

23. In making a report of an accident on a stairway from the mezzanine to the street at a subway station, the LEAST important of the following items to include is the

    A. time of day
    B. number of steps
    C. date
    D. weather

24. Assume that, when you are inspecting one of your assigned stations, you notice a cleaner who in your opinion is under the influence of liquor.
    Your proper procedure is to

    A. let the porter wait in the change booth and check his condition again later
    B. have the porter escorted to the medical office immediately
    C. have the porter sign out sick and send him home
    D. have the railroad clerk verify your judgment

25. A cleaner brings to you, the station supervisor, a passenger who insists he wants to file a claim against the transit authority.
    Your BEST procedure would be to

    A. have the passenger wait while you call the supervisor for instructions
    B. give the passenger an accident report form to fill out
    C. take down the complaint in writing and tell the passenger he will be contacted by an adjuster
    D. direct the passenger to the transit authority claims department

26. A porter on the day trick, who is called in to work four hours in excess ahead of his regular tour of duty will be allowed for his days work a total of

    A. 8 hours plus commensurate time off
    B. 12 hours
    C. 14 hours
    D. 17 hours

27. When a controversial order is issued, the BEST way for a station supervisor to pass the order on to his men is to

    A. briefly discuss the controversial parts
    B. state that he expects the order to be strictly obeyed
    C. suggest it need not be strictly followed
    D. invite their comments

28. It was recently announced that the Transit Authority will conduct a course in courtesy and passenger relations for all railroad clerks and cleaners in the station department. This course is given MAINLY to   28._____

    A. increase subway revenue
    B. assure safety of passengers at all times
    C. improve the quality of service
    D. encourage the public to be more friendly

29. One of your railroad clerks reporting for work on the 7:00 A.M. trick states that he does not feel well. At 8:15 A.M. he claims he is much worse and requests permission to go home. He refuses to go to the medical office and, as he is obviously sick, you allow him to leave.   29._____
    The time that should be charged against his sick leave allowance should be _____ day.

    A. one full   B. 3/4   C. 1/2   D. 1/4

30. Bulletin orders are often reissued without change.   30._____
    The MAIN reason for doing this is to

    A. make sure that the order gets posted on all bulletin boards
    B. replace any lost copies of the order
    C. remind station employees that the order is still in effect
    D. save time in making up a new order

KEY (CORRECT ANSWERS)

1.	B	16.	C
2.	B	17.	D
3.	B	18.	C
4.	A	19.	B
5.	D	20.	B
6.	C	21.	B
7.	A	22.	D
8.	C	23.	B
9.	A	24.	B
10.	B	25.	D
11.	B	26.	C
12.	D	27.	A
13.	B	28.	C
14.	B	29.	B
15.	A	30.	C

EXAMINATION SECTION
TEST 1

DIRECTIONS: Each question or incomplete statement is followed by several suggested answers or completions. Select the one that BEST answers the question or completes the statement. *PRINT THE LETTER OF THE CORRECT ANSWER IN THE SPACE AT THE RIGHT.*

1. In reference to station passes and concession passes, it is *correct* to say that

    A. station passes are not good for transportation
    B. both types of pass must be deposited with the railroad clerk
    C. neither type of pass need be deposited with the railroad clerk
    D. concession passes are not good for transportation

    1.____

2. In giving verbal instructions to a porter, the station supervisor should make them as concise as possible in order to

    A. earn the porter's respect
    B. save the porter's time
    C. impress the porter with the efficiency of transit system procedures
    D. avoid confusing the porter

    2.____

3. After taking over your new assignment as a station supervisor, you find that more of your time than you feel is necessary is spent on maintaining the records turned over to your predecessor.
   You *should*

    A. discontinue for a while those records which you believe are unnecessary and see how this works
    B. work on these records after regular working hours
    C. get together with your station supervisor and decide whether all these records are necessary
    D. assign this part of your duties to a railroad clerk

    3.____

4. At about 3 A.M. on a weekday, a station supervisor notices water pouring into the mezzanine of an express station through a ventilation opening.
   He *should* FIRST

    A. call the trainmaster's office
    B. go to the platform and pull the nearest emergency alarm
    C. go to the street to investigate the cause
    D. call the structure maintenance department

    4.____

5. When a railroad clerk is absent at the time of a pick and has left no choice of job prior to the time of his absence, the supervisor of the pick must select the job for the absent clerk. In studying a job description to make the selection for a clerk whose personal preferences are not known to you, LEAST consideration should be given to

    A. whether the job called for an A.M., or midnight tour
    B. the days specified as the regular days off
    C. whether the job was at a fixed location or was a relief trick
    D. the exact hours specified for reporting and clearing

    5.____

47

6. A station supervisor whose regular tour of duty is from 11 p.m. to 7 a.m. has picked Monday and Tuesday as his regular days off.
   The *total* number of consecutive hours including his days off that this man may be away from his job each week is:

   A. 48   B. 56   C. 64   D. 72

7. The *one* of the following actions which is NOT in violation of the regulations governing newspaper carriers is for the carrier to

   A. throw a small bundle of papers from the train towards a newstand
   B. take a 16 inch x 10 inch x 12 inch bundle into the station
   C. tie his bundles accurately with wire before entering the station
   D. count and sort his papers for delivery while he is riding between stations

8. On a regular school day during the first two thirds of each term, a student with a valid type 2 school eligibility card is required to pay

   A. no train fare either going to school or going home
   B. full fare going to school and none going home
   C. full fare going home and none going to school
   D. five cents for each trip taken in either direction

9. One station of the transit system where there is free transfer among the lines of the three divisions (IND, IRT, BMT) without necessity of going to the street is

   A. City Hall, Manhattan
   B. Broadway-Nassau St., Manhattan
   C. Borough Hall, Brooklyn
   D. Broadway-East New York, Brooklyn

10. A station supervisor noticed a loaded passenger train pulling out of a station with a side door open, and pulled the emergency alarm which was nearby.
    His *next* step should have been to telephone the

    A. trainmaster's office to report the incident
    B. power department to request restoration of power in the station
    C. station department office to request instructions
    D. railroad clerk at the next station to hold the train

11. Some of the men under your supervision present a grievance to you which you know to be common to others who report to other supervisors.
    If you feel that you have found a solution for this grievance satisfactory to your men, you *should*

    A. submit your solution for this grievance through the suggestion program
    B. have the men present the solution to the superintendent through their union representative
    C. try out the solution on your men and then report the results to your supervisor
    D. suggest your solution to the department through the station supervisor

12. A supervisor may justifiably overlook an infraction of the rules which comes to his attention if   12.____

    A. he is off duty when the infraction comes to his notice
    B. the offender will be kept out of trouble by such action
    C. the offender did not harm anyone but himself by this action
    D. the offender committed an offese that was minor and not likely to occur again

13. An acquaintance who knows your position in the transit system complains to you that the   13.____
    stairway he uses to enter the subway each morning is littered with discarded cigarette butts and wrappers and points this out as an example of inefficiency. You know the entrance referred to is very heavily used during the morning rush hours and that many passengers do discard cigarettes there.
    In the interest of good public relations, the most helpful response from you would be to

    A. say nothing so as not to antagonize your acquaintance
    B. point out that it is impracticable for the porter to clear the litter until after the rush hour
    C. suggest that your acquaintance should file a formal complaint with the Transit Authority
    D. tell your acquaintance that you will order the porter to pay more attention to this stairway

14. Assume that you have been ordered to see that the turnstiles at a certain station   14.____
    entrance are closed to passengers because of a long train delay due to a flood. While you are there, a photographer approaches you, displays his press card, and asks to be permitted to enter the station.
    Your proper response after checking the press card is to

    A. admit him without further question
    B. refer him to the station superintendent's office
    C. have him sign a release and then admit him
    D. refer him to the transit police bureau

15. In the preceding situation, passengers who are inside the turnstiles and who desire to   15.____
    leave and have their fares refunded are issues block tickets.
    One sound reason for issuing block tickets rather than cash in such a situation is that

    A. there can never be enough cash on hand
    B. too many people would leave if cash were refunded
    C. the law requires their use
    D. normal cash reserves are interfered with

16. A station supervisor is told by a train dispatcher that a certain interval is to be   16.____
    dropped.
    This means that

    A. the time interval between certain trains is to be reduced
    B. a certain train is to be taken out of service and no substitute made
    C. a certain train is to be reduced in length by a specified number of cars
    D. an additional train is to be placed on service in the interval between two regularly scheduled trains

17. A station supervisor who is off duty notices two passengers engaged in a fist fight on a station mezzanine. In this case, he would do *best* to

    A. take no action but be ready to render assistance, if necessary, when the fighting stops
    B. try to find a transit employee who is on duty and tell him to separate the fighters
    C. try to talk the men out of fighting without becoming physically involved himself
    D. send someone to summon the transit police while he tries to pull the fighters apart

18. Certain lost articles are required to be forwarded to the station department office by special messenger as soon as possible before being turned in. One such lost article would be a

    A. wallet containing considerable money
    B. switchblade knife
    C. hamper of fish
    D. press-type camera loaded with film

19. A package is offered to a porter by the passenger who found it. Before accepting the package, the porter is required to first

    A. obtain the passenger's name and address
    B. offer to give the passenger a receipt
    C. take the passenger to the nearest booth so as to have a witness
    D. offer to escort the passenger to the nearest 24-booth to get a receipt

20. Three Manhattan stations of the New York City Transit Authority are called "Fifth Avenue." These stations are at 5th Ave., and

    A. 14th, 23rd, and 34th Streets
    B. 23rd, 34th, and 42nd Streets
    C. 34th, 42nd, and 53rd Streets
    D. 42nd, 53rd, and 60th Streets

21. Assume that a new sports stadium has been built near one of the stations of the transit system, and that a large attendance is expected on opening day.
    In this case, the number of people who are likely to use the transit system when the opening day's sporting event is over can *best* be determined by

    A. obtaining the official attendance figure and applying a percentage based on previous experience
    B. assuming there will be a capacity attendance and that 40% to 50% will use the transit system
    C. subtracting 1.75 times the number of automobiles in the parking area from the official attendance figure
    D. making a count of the passengers leaving the station during the two hours preceding the event and assuming that approximately this number will return

22. A person wishing to travel from Borough Hall, Brooklyn, to City Hall, Manhattan, will come *closest* to his destination by using the

    A. IND Concourse express   B. IND 8th Ave. express
    C. BMT Brighton express   D. IRT Lexington Ave. express

23. The rules and regulations specify the maximum length of a train that may be operated in passenger service on any part of the transit system. One reason for limiting the maximum length of train by rule is that

    A. longer trains would cause excessive strain on drawbars
    B. traffic does not warrant longer trains
    C. many station platforms will not accomodate longer trains
    D. conductors cannot be expected to control more doors

23.____

24. Drop safes are used in change booths instead of other types of safes mainly because drop safes

    A. permit railroad clerks to deposit revenue but not to remove it
    B. make it easier for the collection agents
    C. cannot be left open accidentally
    D. can be built into the wall and so cannot be removed

24.____

25. When checking over a particular porter's schedule for possible revisions, it is NOT necessary to take into consideration whether the

    A. passenger traffic entering and exiting is well spread out over the day or is highly concentrated
    B. porter is a new man or has had years of experience
    C. station involved is in a factory or residential area
    D. passengers generally traverse a large or small part of the station area

25.____

26. A station supervisor receives a telephone report from a station department employee that a stair tread is defective. The primary interest of the assistant station supervisor *should* be to

    A. see if there are other defective treads on the stairway
    B. determine if this defect was reported previously
    C. have the tread repaired promptly
    D. fix responsibility for damage

26.____

27. Suppose that you are a station supervisor and assign three porters to a special clean-up job which does not require your continuous presence. To get the *best* results, you should

    A. tell the three porters they are each equally responsible for the entire job
    B. designate one of the porters to be in charge of the job when you are away
    C. instruct the porters to keep in touch with you frequently
    D. tell each porter he is responsible for only his part of the work

27.____

28. As a station supervisor, one of the best ways to cooperate with your supervisor would be to

    A. immediately report to him every infraction of the rules which you observe
    B. continually report all details of the work under your supervision
    C. make frequent suggestions for changes in work schedules
    D. accept full responsibility for the work assigned to you

28.____

29. It would be necessary for a station supervisor to obtain approval from his supervisor before

    A. arranging with his relief to leave an hour earlier the next day
    B. calling the transit police in an emergency
    C. giving one of his porter's a deserved reprimand
    D. giving a railroad clerk relief because of unusual conditions

30. A station supervisor observing an unusually large influx of passengers at one of his stations on several successive days would do best, as a first step, to

    A. assign several light-duty men to this station to make a traffic count
    B. contact the general manager's office to inquire as to the cause
    C. examine the area adjacent to the station to see whether there have been changes in surface transportation or housing
    D. note this fact daily on the combined railroad clerks daily fare report until a pattern has been established

31. If a station supervisor hears a long-short-long-short whistle signal from a train which is entering the station, the *best* of the following moves for him to make is to

    A. go to the train and investigate
    B. pull the emergency alarm
    C. notify the signal maintainer
    D. notify the car inspector

32. One function of the emergency alarm system in the subway is to

    A. restore power to the third rail in an emergency
    B. provide a means of communication in the event of a power failure
    C. supply power to the emergency tunnel lights
    D. sound an alarm at a designated headquarters

33. Of the following, the BEST way to have transit employees, as a whole, learn good safety habits is to

    A. let them learn through their own mistakes
    B. offer prizes for the best safety records
    C. have them study the rules during their spare time
    D. penalize them with loss of pay for lost-time accidents

34. A railroad clerk who works 7 a.m. to 3 p.m. in a 24-hour revenue booth should be instructed to enter on his time card

    A. 8 hrs. regular time plus 15 minutes check-out time allowance
    B. 8 hrs. regular time plus 10 minutes check-out time allowance
    C. 8 hrs. regular time plus 5 minutes check-out time allowance
    D. 8 hrs. regular time plus no check-out time allowance

35. If, when picking up supplies at a storeroom, a porter requests a new mop but does not have a used one to turn in, the proper procedure for the assistant station supervisor in charge of issuing supplies is to

A. deny the request
B. issue a new mop without question
C. find out what happened to the old one
D. telephone the station department office for instruction

36. A supervisor who is performing his job well should be checking all operations under his jurisdiction.
Of the following, the MOST important reason for doing this is to make certain that

    A. he personally observes all operations as they are performed
    B. all the operations are still needed
    C. subordinates are performing their work efficiently
    D. operations are being performed as scheduled

36._____

37. A certificate for free transportation of a group of children, when presented to a railroad clerk, need NOT have entered on it before presentation the

    A. serial number
    B. maximum number of children covered
    C. destination of the group
    D. intended time of return

37._____

38. A station supervisor on a 7 a.m. to 3 p.m. tour notices that a regular passenger passageway in the subway is completely dark.
The *proper* procedure for him would be to notify the

    A. light maintainer   B. station superintendent
    C. porter   D. zone field office

38._____

39. Assume that, soon after you are appointed as an assistant station supervisor, an experienced assistant station supervisor tells you that you are not making out certain reports according to standard procedures.
In this case, you should give his criticism due consideration because the elder man

    A. will not help you in the future if his admonition is ignored
    B. is in a position to enforce his criticism
    C. had had more experience on the job
    D. is likely to report you if you do not change your procedure

39._____

40. Stationery and cleaning supplies for each station are picked up by the porters on the day tour every

    A. week from one of the 20 field storerooms
    B. two weeks from one of the four main storerooms
    C. two weeks from one of the 20 field storerooms
    D. week from one of the 4 main storerooms

40._____

KEY (CORRECT ANSWERS)

1. A	11. D	21. D	31. A
2. D	12. D	22. D	32. D
3. C	13. B	23. C	33. B
4. C	14. A	24. A	34. A
5. D	15. D	25. B	35. C
6. C	16. B	26. C	36. B
7. B	17. C	27. B	37. D
8. C	18. A	28. D	38. D
9. B	19. D	29. A	39. C
10. A	20. D	30. C	40. C

TEST 2

DIRECTIONS: Each question or incomplete statement is followed by several suggested answers or completions. Select the one that BEST answers the question or completes the statement. *PRINT THE LETTER OF THE CORRECT ANSWER IN THE SPACE AT THE RIGHT.*

QUESTIONS 1-7.

Questions 1-7, inclusive, are based on the tabulation of Turnstile Readings shown in the chart below. Consult this tabulation in answering these questions.
NOTE that booth No. 222 is open 24 hours a day; the clerk on the midnight tour reporting at 11:00 p.m.

TURNSTILE READING
BOOTH NO. 222 - ECKS ST. STA.
Monday - September 8

HOUR	TURNSTILE NUMBER				
	1	2	3	4	5
5 AM	88782	81365	33627	42819	12633
6 AM	88916	81517	33755	42936	12745
7 AM	88388	82051	34203	43345	13137
8 AM	90005	83875	35736	44749	14476
9 AM	91828	85936	37469	46328	15988
10 AM	92503	86687	38106	46911	16546
11 AM	92908	87143	38490	47262	16882
12 NOON	93297	87581	38869	47607	17213
1 PM	93694	88024	39251	47956	17542
2 PM	94093	88472	39626	48303	17875
3 PM	94627	89071	40128	48761	18316
4 PM	95269	89799	40770	49346	18871
5 PM	96484	91167	41922	50399	19879
6 PM	98595	93514	43914	52202	21630
7 PM	99486	94517	44759	52974	22369
8 PM	99945	95034	45194	53372	22750
9 PM	00256	95384	45489	53653	23008

1. Of the listed turnstile readings, the one which should definitely appear on the regular combined railroad clerks daily fare report is

    A. 83875   B. 89071   C. 94093   D. 95384

    1.____

2. The MOST probable of the following conclusions which may be drawn from the given information is that the

    A. counter of turnstile #5 has recently been replaced
    B. most used stairway from the street is nearest turnstile #2
    C. turnstiles are on the same level as the train platform
    D. change booth is close to the foot of one of the stairways from the street

    2.____

55

3. The average number of passengers per minute using turnstile #2 during the busiest hour was *nearest* to

   A. 34   B. 35   C. 39   D. 41

4. If turnstile #2 had been closed from 9 a.m. to 2 p.m. while the total number of passenger traffic remained the same, and the passengers that would have used turnstile #2 were divided equally among the other four turnstiles, the readings of turnstile #4 at 5 p.m. would have been

   A. 49765   B. 49980   C. 51033   D. 51568

5. The total number of passengers using turnstile #5 during the entire period from 5 a.m. to 9 p.m. was less than the number of passengers using turnstile #2 during the 11-hour period from

   A. 5 a.m. to 4 p.m.
   B. 6 a.m. to 5 p.m.
   C. 8 a.m. to 7 p.m.
   D. 10 a.m. to 9 p.m.

6. If 25% of the passengers entering through these turnstiles in 24 hours were registered in the two hours from 7 a.m. to 9 a.m., the total number of passengers registered this day was *approximately*

   A. 41,000   B. 49,000   C. 66,000   D. 69,000

7. From your knowledge of passenger traffic flow at rapid transit stations in New York City, you would be justified in concluding that the tabulation would apply most nearly to a station having the characteristics of

   A. Wall St.
   B. Grand Central
   C. Columbus Circle
   D. Coney Island

8. One station of the transit system where there is NOT a free transfer between lines of two different divisions is

   A. Chamber St., on the IND Division
   B. Cortlandt St., on the BMT Division
   C. Brooklyn Bridge on the IRT Division
   D. Fulton St., on the BMT Division

9. A certain porter sweeps the station very thoroughly when it is swept, but does not sweep as often as called for on the schedule.
   Under these circumstances it would be *best* for the assistant station supervisor to

   A. insist that the porter follow the schedule
   B. assign the porter to less desirable cleaning tasks
   C. revise this porter's cleaning schedule to agree with the work being done
   D. overlook the situation because the sweeping is satisfactorily done

10. One of your porters was injured as a result of slipping on a wet scrub brush while in the process of washing a wall. This accident probably could have been prevented if the porter had

    A. used equipment which was not defective
    B. followed proper housekeeping procedures

C. been in good physical condition
D. worn proper safety shoes

11. Assume that a station supervisor is required by his superiors to transmit an order with which he does not agree, to the railroad clerks under his supervision. In this case, the assistant station supervisor should properly

    A. ask one of his superiors to transmit the order because he does not agree with it
    B. tell his superiors that he will not transmit the order because he does not agree with it
    C. transmit the order and carefully explain it to the rail road clerks that he does not agree with it
    D. transmit the order and enforce it to the best of his ability

11.____

12. Using transit system telephone numbered M3-456 to call transit system telephone numbered Bl-234, the proper procedure is to remove the receiver, wait for the dial tone, and dial

    A. B1-234   B. MZ1-234   C. BZ1-234   D. Z1-234

12.____

13. If you, a station supervisor on duty, notice a stranger in street clothes walk off a subway platform onto the benchwalk, your BEST procedure would be to

    A. assume the stranger to be a transit employee and take no action
    B. warn the motorman of the next train to operate cautiously because there is a man in the tunnel
    C. telephone the transit police and report the incident
    D. call to the stranger and ask to see his identification

13.____

14. If it is extremely important to be certain that all railclerks have seen a temporary special order, the BEST procedure would be to

    A. have the station supervisor go to each booth and read the order to the railroad clerks
    B. have the order state that each railroad clerk should confirm by calling the station supervisor's office
    C. put the name of every railroad clerk on the order and post it on the bulletin boards
    D. have each railroad clerk return a signed copy of the order to the office

14.____

15. When inspecting a stairway where a passenger has fallen, it is NOT necessary to check the

    A. tightness of handrails   B. wear of the steps
    C. height of risers   D. condition of light bulbs

15.____

16. A railroad clerk who regularly works from 7 a.m. to 3 p.m. in a 24-hour booth is relieved at 3:40 p.m. by a relief clerk because his regular relief did not report. His pay for this day will be at his regular rate for

    A. 8 hours, 40 minutes   B. 8 hours, 45 minutes
    C. 9 hours, 55 minutes   D. 9 hours

16.____

17. A railroad clerk who works his regular tour from 11 p.m. to 7 a.m. in a 24-hour booth and then works 8 a.m. to 11 a.m. on an overtime assignment will be paid for this day's work at his regular rate for

    A. 12 hours, 25 minutes
    B. 12 hours, 30 minutes
    C. 12 hours, 40 minutes
    D. 12 hours, 45 minutes

17.___

18. To train the porters on your section in the use of a new cleaning material for which the printed instructions and the cleaning procedure are exceptionally complicated, the BEST of the following methods is to

    A. arrange to have the entire group of porters witness a demonstration by the supplier of the cleaning material at one of your stations
    B. issue a copy of the cleaning material supplier's printed instructions to each porter and tell him to follow the instructions
    C. arrange to have one porter trained by the supplier of the cleaning material and have him instruct the others
    D. learn the procedure yourself and then instruct the porters in small groups on the job

18.___

19. The station supervisor requests you to survey the stations under your supervision for the purpose of determining the best locations for litter baskets. In preparing a written report of your survey, the first part of the report following a short introduction should be a

    A. description of your survey procedures
    B. list of the recommended basket locations
    C. sketch of the territory surveyed
    D. list of the present basket locations

19.___

20. In the preceding question, the report should be addressed to the

    A. station supervisor
    B. station superintendent
    C. assistant general superintendent
    D. general manager

20.___

21. If you, a station supervisor, saw a line of passengers waiting at an auxiliary rush-hour railroad clerk's booth while the clerk was retrieving fare cards, your PROPER procedure would be to

    A. ask the clerk whether the shortage occurred often
    B. note this occurence and enter it upon the clerk's record
    C. step into the booth and sell tokens until the clerk returned
    D. transfer 500 fare cards from the adjacent regular booth

21.___

22. If you were is the Times Square mezzanine inside the turnstiles when a passenger asked you for the quickest way to reach the Empire State Building, you should tell him to ride the

    A. BMT to 34th St.
    B. IRT to Penn. Sta.
    C. IRT to Fifth Ave.
    D. IND to Fifth Ave.

22.___

23. The best way to be sure that a railroad clerk will make proper entries on a new printed form for which written instructions have been distributed, is to have the clerk

   A. watch the assistant station supervisor make the entries a few times and then try it himself
   B. attend an instruction class on the subject with other railroad clerks
   C. consult with a more experienced clerk at a nearby booth when making the entries
   D. fill in the form at his assigned location and then let the assistant station supervisor examine it for errors

24. Part of the time of supervision is required in investigating complaints by passengers against employees. The BEST of the following suggested overall solutions to this problem is to

   A. educate passengers to the fact that investigating complaints is expensive
   B. send a standard courteous answer and omit investigation
   C. have superiors stress courtesy in public relations
   D. investigate only the legitimate complaints

25. You are informed by the station supervisor that one of the stations under your supervision has been reported to be in very dirty condition. In this case, your BEST procedure is to

   A. call up the railroad clerk on duty, asking him to investigate and telephone you immediately
   B. call up the railroad clerk on duty and have him send the porter in to the office for investigation
   C. go to the station and inspect it personally
   D. ask the station supervisor if he has verified the report

26. A passenger has fallen on the subway station platform and broken his leg. While awaiting the ambulance, an assistant station supervisor should make the passenger as comfortable as possible and then

   A. go to the edge of the platform to flag down oncoming trains
   B. try to obtain the identity of the injured person and the names of witnesses
   C. apply temporary splints
   D. leave the injured person in the hands of a platform man and go about his duties

27. If a passenger train carrying considerably less than a normal load is followed by a train carrying considerably more than a normal load for that particular time of day, it is *most likely* that

   A. the first train is on time and the second is behind schedule
   B. the first train is ahead of schedule and the second is on time
   C. both trains are ahead of schedule
   D. both trains are behind schedule

28. In evaluating the services of a railroad clerk, the station supervisor would be *most effectively* guided by the clerk's

   A. general dependability
   B. willingness to accept the least desirable trick

C. sick leave record
D. willingness to work overtime

29. Railroad clerks working in certain booths on the midnight tour are required to prepare daily reports of fare registrations and net fares as soon as practicable after reporting for duty.
The BEST reason for having the midnight clerks (rather than the a.m. or p.m. clerks) prepare these daily reports is that the

    A. midnight clerks are not as busy as the others
    B. most experienced clerks are assigned to midnight tours
    C. regular mail pick-up and delivery takes place shortly after midnight
    D. information for the entire day is not available on the earlier tour

30. A man approaches you in a subway mezzanine and tells you that he has tried to purchase 20 fares from the railroad clerk, offering a fifty-dollar bill in payment, but that the railroad clerk would not sell the fares because the bill that was tendered was larger than twenty dollars. The man says that the railroad clerk referred him to you.
It would probably be BEST for you to

    A. explain to him that such large purchases can only be made at Jay St. headquarters
    B. suggest that he should go to a nearby store and change the bill
    C. accompany the man to the booth and advise the clerk to sell him the fares, taking normal precautions against counterfeit money
    D. change the bill for the man yourself, after taking his name and address

31. In the course of making your rounds one morning about 11 a.m., you find a full-time subway booth unmanned, the door locked, the lights on, and a line of people waiting to buy tokens. The first person in line tells you that the clerk went upstairs about 10 minutes ago saying he'd be "right back."
Your *best* course of action is to sell tokens to the waiting passengers and then

    A. lock the booth and look for the clerk
    B. report the situation to the station department office
    C. notify the transit police
    D. locate the porter and have him look for the clerk

32. There is no rapid transit line crossing the East River from Manhattan at

    A. Houston St.   B. Delancey St.
    C. Fulton St.   D. Whitehall St.

33. If a station supervisor observes one of his porters doing a cleaning job in an unsatisfactory manner, the assistant station supervisor should

    A. show the porter the approved way to do the work before allowing him to continue
    B. wait until the cleaning is finished and then show the porter the approved method
    C. reprimand the porter and then show the porter a new assigned work
    D. make a note of it and take action only if such unsatisfactory work is repeated

34. Assume that a station supervisor is told by a railroad clerk that something blew into his eye and is causing him considerable pain. Of the following, the most *desirable* action for the station supervisor to take is to

    A. look for the dirt particle and try to get it out
    B. relieve the clerk a few minutes while he tries to remove the dirt
    C. telephone for a relief and send the clerk to the clinic
    D. send the clerk home and use the porter for relief

35. Your investigation of an accident in a station would be MOST fruitful if

    A. you find that the transit authority was not responsible
    B. information was obtained which might prevent similar accidents in the future
    C. you found it was the fault of another department
    D. the responsibility could be pinned on a specific employee

36. The establishment of cleaning gangs for major cleaning operations together with the assignment of 2 or 3 stations per porter for routine operations, is *primarily* for the purpose of

    A. improving overall responsibility for work more accurately
    B. improving overall work efficiency
    C. increasing the individual porter's pride of workmanship
    D. insuring better coverage in emergencies

37. A limping female passenger is escorted to you by the porter at one of your stations. She complains to you that she slipped on the cleaning compound being used by the porter and as a result, she fell, bruising her knees and tearing her stockings.
    It would show good judgment on your part if you

    A. offered to provide medical assistance
    B. reprimand the porter on the spot
    C. suggested that she should file a formal complaint
    D. told her to go home and wait for a claim adjuster

38. If large numbers of slugs were found in the turnstiles at a station having only mechanical turnstiles, the *first* step to be taken by the station supervisor to help apprehend the guilty parties would be to

    A. assign additional station department personnel to watch the turnstiles
    B. request the transit police bureau to assign detectives
    C. spot-check the turnstiles himself at irregular intervals
    D. have the railroad clerk retrieve and check the contents of each turnstile hourly

39. There is no direct subway route between

    A. Queens and Brooklyn
    B. Queens and the Bronx
    C. Manhattan and the Bronx
    D. Manhattan and Brooklyn

40. The maximum number of unused AVA days which an hourly rated employee may have to his credit at any one time is

    A. 2   B. 4   C. 6   D. 8

KEY (CORRECT ANSWERS)

1. C	11. D	21. A	31. B
2. B	12. A	22. A	32. A
3. C	13. D	23. D	33. A
4. C	14. D	24. C	34. C
5. C	15. C	25. C	35. B
6. C	16. B	26. B	36. B
7. B	17. C	27. B	37. A
8. B	18. D	28. A	38. D
9. A	19. B	29. D	39. B
10. B	20. A	30. C	40. C

EXAMINATION SECTION
TEST 1

DIRECTIONS: Each question or incomplete statement is followed by several suggested answers or completions. Select the one that BEST answers the question or completes the statement. *PRINT THE LETTER OF THE CORRECT ANSWER IN THE SPACE AT THE RIGHT.*

1. As a station supervisor, if you think of a means for controlling passengers at the foot of a station escalator, your BEST procedure would be to

    A. get the opinion of the subway employees assigned to the station
    B. discuss it with an assistant supervisor of the elevator and escalator department
    C. ask your supervisor for the assignment of sufficient personnel to give the plan a trial before recommending it
    D. consider the idea carefully before recommending it

2. Before giving a conductor on the train the proper hand signal to close the doors, the conductor assigned to platform duty should ascertain whether

    A. the scheduled time for departure has arrived
    B. all waiting passengers are aboard
    C. a connecting train is approaching
    D. all doors are opened

3. Courtesy to passengers is constantly impressed on subway employees *mainly* to

    A. improve public relations
    B. increase the use of subways by the public
    C. minimize operating difficulties
    D. assure the safety of the passengers

4. An excited passenger, just inside the turnstiles, calls out something to the railroad clerk in the booth which he cannot understand.
   The *best* course of action for the clerk to take would be to

    A. ignore the passenger until he comes over to the booth
    B. close the booth and go over to the turnstiles to investigate
    C. tell the passenger he will get help for him
    D. tell the passenger to calm down so he can understand

5. A thorough knowledge of the schedule of working conditions for employees in the station department will help an assistant station supervisor to know

    A. how to tell whether a porter is doing a satisfactory job
    B. when one of his subordinates should be reprimanded
    C. if certain of his duties can be delegated to one of his subordinates
    D. what monetary rights his subordinates have

6. A station supervisor will find that it is sometimes more effective to warn a subordinate than to institute action for more severe punishment, because

    A. the warning is less severe
    B. the punishment is often inappropriate
    C. the warning may produce a more cooperative attitude
    D. a warning always creates a better impression than punishment

7. One of your workers, when reporting to work, claims he is not feeling well. After working just over an hour, he requests permission to go home as he is feeling worse. He refuses to have medical attention, and, since he is obviously sick, he is allowed to leave.
In this case, the time charged against his sick leave allowance should be

   A. 1/4 day   B. 1/2 day   C. 3/4 day   D. a full day

8. CO_2 type fire extinguishers are mounted on tunnel walls. In order to have them available for any emergency it is especially essential that

   A. they be frequently replaced
   B. they be periodically inspected
   C. only designated persons should use them
   D. prompt notice be given whenever they are used

9. One of your railroad clerks asks you to grant him a minor privilege. In granting or denying such a request, you should consider

   A. that all such requests should be denied
   B. the clerk's seniority
   C. the merits of the case
   D. that it is bad for employees morale to grant a request of this nature

10. The revenue department is nost desirous that railroad clerks be very careful when handling revenue because errors in bagging

    A. are difficult to detect
    B. increase the department's work load
    C. reflect on the railroad clerks honesty
    D. result in erroneous reports of daily receipts

11. A conductor assigned to platform duty is expected to

    A. normally remain on duty until relieved
    B. prevent anyone from loitering in or around the change booth
    C. gently push a person into a crowded car so the doors can close
    D. stop people running from trains to stairways

12. Certain types of lost property found on the transit system should be held for 12 hours and then either sold or destroyed. Such an article would be a

    A. broken umbrella   B. bottle of liquor
    C. basket of fruit   D. thermos bottle full of milk

13. As a result of a recent safety bulletin, a certain railroad porter has taken upon himself the duty of thoroughly inspecting his assigned territory for any condition which he thinks requires any repairs or painting and is constantly reporting such information to the station supervisor.
The most *effective* means of dealing with such a situation is to

    A. have a talk with the porter and explain just what is expected of him
    B. disregard the reports until the porter realizes that he is making a nuisance of himself
    C. recommend giving him a special assignment of inspecting all the stations under the supervision of this assistant station supervisor
    D. get tough with the porter and insist he pay more attention to his assigned work

14. If a new method of bagging revenue were to be started at a certain station, the station supervisor desiring to minimize errors should

    A. know that considerable time may be required for employees to become familiar with the procedure
    B. realize that frequent mistakes are possible
    C. keep this station under close supervision
    D. do the initial bagging himself

14.____

15. A certain cleaner, while working under your supervision, swept the station very thoroughly when it was swept but did not sweep as often as necessary. Shortly after picking a different station his new station supervisor asks your opinion of the cleaner.
Your *best* course of action would be to

    A. point out the man's good qualities only
    B. point out the man's faults only
    C. point out both his good and his poor characteristics
    D. avoid committing yourself in order to give him a chance at a new station

15.____

QUESTIONS 16-21.

Questions 16 to 21 are based on the situation described below. Consider the facts given in this situation when answering these questions.

Assume that at a certain subway station a complete traffic count is to be taken on May 26th for a period of 24 hours. A total of 15 employees are assigned to make the count under the general supervision of a station supervisor, assisted by 3 "light duty" train operators.

16. The verbal instructions given to the assigned counters by the station supervisor should be as brief and concise as possible in order to

    A. avoid confusing the counters
    B. emphasize the importance of the instructions
    C. get the count started as soon as possible
    D. be effective

16.____

17. The most *probable* reason for assigning the motormen as assistants is that they

    A. have a higher title than the counters
    B. are experienced in such work
    C. can be depended on to prepare reports correctly
    D. receive more training than the other employees

17.____

18. If the largest number of counters are assigned to work between 5 a.m. and 8 a.m., this would *most likely* indicate that the station is located

    A. in a residential area   B. in a manufacturing district
    C. at a shopping center   D. at a railroad terminal

18.____

19. To accomplish the purpose for which it is intended, such a traffic count should be conducted

    A. frequently
    B. by experienced people
    C. with accuracy
    D. only at congested stations

20. The reason for assigning so many employees to this task is *most likely* due to

    A. their inexperience
    B. the number of people using this station
    C. the impracticable way in which this count is taken
    D. the physical layout of the station

21. The *least probable* reason for conducting such a count is to

    A. determine when the station is the most crowded
    B. determine if additional turnstiles are needed
    C. make a comparison between the number of people leaving the station and those entering the station
    D. determine the "flow" of passengers at certain stairways

22. Many accidents could be prevented if employees remember that safety rules

    A. will be strictly enforced
    B. should be learned
    C. are often used and based on previous accidents
    D. should be obeyed

23. All employee training courses are beneficial to the system because such courses

    A. tend to increase employee efficiency
    B. prepare employees for promotional examinations
    C. are given by people well acquainted with the work
    D. increase the interest of new employees

24. A station agent in a booth is notified by the station supervisor that a special relief is being sent to permit the clerk to come to his office.
    When the relief arrives, it is *most important* that the station agent should

    A. make certain the booth is locked before he leaves
    B. not admit the man to the booth unless certain of his identity
    C. notify his superior of the relief's arrival
    D. inform the station porter that he is going to the office

25. A station agent noticing that a post light cannot be turned off should make an immediate report to his office *primarily* to

    A. have repairs made promptly
    B. avoid criticism by his superior
    C. find out what the trouble is
    D. determine if this defect was previously reported

26. A station agent may exchange tokens for as many as 4 regular cash fare tickets when presented by a passenger, but is only permitted to exchange one token for a single special (red) cash fare ticket issued by the Board of Education for an elementary school pupil.
 The *most probable* reason for limiting the exchange to a single ticket issued for school pupils is to

 A. minimize the possibility of the school tickets being used illegally
 B. prevent the school tickets from being stolen
 C. insure that the school ticket is only used by the one to whom issued
 D. enable the railroad clerk to check that the school ticket had been regularly issued

26._____

27. A station agent in a change booth should be most interested in the fact that a child under 6 years traveling with an adult is

 A. liable to break away from the adult and dash under the turnstile
 B. not to occupy a seat to the exclusion of an adult
 C. the responsibility of the adult he accompanies
 D. to be carried free of charge

27._____

28. To frustrate holdups, station agents are instructed

 A. as to the time holdups usually occur
 B. to be careful lest perpetrators be armed
 C. as to the general appearance of holdup men
 D. to keep booth doors locked

28._____

29. The most significant argument against making it compulsory for civil service employees to attend a training course is

 A. trainees must be receptive if training is to be successful
 B. most training requires additional time and expense on the part of the trainee
 C. unwilling trainees will be penalized in any event by non-promotion
 D. training is highly desirable, but not absolutely essential, for adequate job performance

29._____

30. A station employee should NOT enter upon the subway tracks without first

 A. notifying another employee where he is going
 B. checking to make sure that no trains are coming
 C. having someone stationed to warn him of approaching trains
 D. obtaining the required flagging protection

30._____

KEY (CORRECT ANSWERS)

1.	D	16.	A
2.	B	17.	A
3.	A	18.	B
4.	D	19.	C
5.	D	20.	D
6.	C	21.	C
7.	C	22.	D
8.	D	23.	A
9.	C	24.	B
10.	B	25.	A
11.	A	26.	A
12.	C	27.	D
13.	A	28.	D
14.	C	29.	A
15.	C	30.	B

TEST 2

DIRECTIONS: Each question or incomplete statement is followed by several suggested answers or completions. Select the one that BEST answers the question or completes the statement. *PRINT THE LETTER OF THE CORRECT ANSWER IN THE SPACE AT THE RIGHT.*

QUESTIONS 1-10.

Questions 1-10 contain working schedules that refer to the column of time allowances shown below. Select the proper time allowance in the column which should be used with the working schedule given in each question.

Column of time allowances

A.	8 hr. 00 min.	M.	9 hr. 15 min.
B.	8 hr. 15 min.	O.	9 hr. 30 min.
C.	8 hr. 20 min.	P.	9 hr. 45 min.
D.	8 hr. 30 min.	S.	10 hr. 00 min.
E.	8 hr. 40 min.	T.	10 hr. 30 min.
H.	8 hr. 45 min.	V.	11 hr. 00 min.
J.	9 hr. 00 min.	X.	11 hr. 30 min.
K.	9 hr. 10 min.		

1. A railroad clerk reported at 8:00 A.M., was relieved at 11:30 A.M., resumed work at 11:55 A.M. and went home at 4:00 P.M. He was told to phone his office at 5:30 P.M. for possible emergency work. He did so but was told he was not needed. 1.____

2. A station employee reported at 3:00 P.M., was relieved for lunch at 7:00 P.M., resumed work at 7:30 P.M., and was relieved at 11:00 P.M. 2.____

3. A station employee reported at 8:00 A.M., was relieved for lunch at 12:15 P.M. and resumed work at 12:40 P.M. His relief failed to arrive at 4:00 P.M. as scheduled so he had to work until relieved at 4:30 P.M. 3.____

4. A cleaner reported at 8:00 A.M., went to lunch at 1:00 P.M., resumed work at 3:40 P.M., worked until 6:30 P.M. 4.____

5. A station employee reported at 6:00 A.M., was relieved at 11:30 A.M., resumed work at 12:00 Noon and was relieved at 2:00 P.M. He was told to come back at 4:00 P.M. for emergency work. When he did so, he was told he was not needed. 5.____

6. A cleaner reported at 6:00 A.M., went to lunch at 10:30 A.M., resumed work at 10:40 A.M. because of an emergency, and worked until 2:00 P.M. 6.____

7. A station employee reported at 5:00 A.M., was relieved at 9:45 A.M., resumed work at 10:10 A.M. Relief failed to arrive at 1:00 P.M. as scheduled, so he worked until relieved at 1:50 P.M. 7.____

8. A station employee reported at 8:00 A.M., was relieved at 11:45 A.M., resumed at 12:15 P.M., and was relieved at 4:00 P.M. He reported back as directed at 5:30 P.M., put to work, and released at 6:30 P.M. 8.____

9. A station employee reported at 11:00 P.M., was relieved at 4:00 A.M. and resumed work at 4:30 A.M. Relief failed to arrive at 7:00 A.M. as scheduled, so he had to work until relieved at 8:10 A.M. 9.____

69

10. A cleaner reported at 7:00 A.M., went to lunch at 12:30 P.M., resumed at 1:45 P.M., and worked until 4:15 P.M.

11. One of your cleaners was injured as a result of slipping on a wet spot on the station platform. This type of accident would *most likely* be classified as due to

    A. defective equipment
    B. poor housekeeping
    C. physical condition
    D. proper safety appliances not used

12. A cleaner, who is a habitual complainer, presents a grievance which has some merit. As a station supervisor, you should handle this grievance by

    A. ignoring it
    B. recommending unfavorable action
    C. referring it to your supervisor
    D. adjusting it if possible

13. A characteristic which a station supervisor should consider most desirable in his subordinates is the

    A. willingness to report back to the assistant supervisor all disparaging remarks made by the employees
    B. desire to put in as much overtime as possible
    C. ability to refrain from talking with passengers
    D. ability to properly carry out assignments with a minimum of instructions

14. Air raid sirens are located at various stations on the transit system. Railroad clerks at these locations are instructed to note the time at which test signals are received at their location. The main reason for those time notations is

    A. to test time clocks on the system
    B. that the sirens throughout the city be synchronized
    C. too see if the railroad clerks are alert
    D. that the same signal is received at all locations

15. It would be poor supervision if a station supervisor

    A. consulted his supervisor on personnel problems
    B. made it a policy to avoid criticism of his subordinates in front of passengers
    C. allowed a cooling-off period of several days before giving one of his subordinates a deserved reprimand
    D. asked an experienced porter for his opinion of a suggested method for cleaning tile

16. You believe that a conductor assigned to platform duty at one of your stations shirks his duty whenever possible. To ascertain the validity of your belief it would be *best* for you to

    A. make several unscheduled visits to the location
    B. question the railroad clerk on duty at the station
    C. question the conductor to see if he knows what his duties are
    D. dispatch another employee to check on the conductor

17. A station supervisor criticizing a cleaner's work expresses disappointment, stating that not only is his work entirely unsatisfactory, but that his accident record is also bad.
    The station supervisor's method of handling this situation would usually be considered

    A. poor; the cleaner should have been asked why his work was poor
    B. poor; some favorable comment should have been made at the same time
    C. good; it is advisable to keep this type of interview as short as possible
    D. good; the cleaner will realize that his work will have to improve if he is to keep his job

17._____

18. Whenever an employee under your supervision has an accident on the job, you, as a station supervisor, are *required* to

    A. make sure that the employee prepares and submits an accident report before the completion of his tour of duty
    B. prepare and submit a "supervisory accident report" before the completion of your tour of duty
    C. immediately investigate and give an oral report to your supervisor
    D. recommend means to prevent a repetition of the accident

18._____

19. At stations where additional personnel are required to sell fares, the exact location where the seller stands is determined primarily by

    A. its proximity to the change booth
    B. the lighting in the station
    C. the line of flow of traffic
    D. the number of passengers using the station

19._____

20. When a bulletin order is reissued without change, the purpose of this *usually* is to

    A. supersede prior bulletins
    B. stress its importance
    C. make sure the order reaches all bulletin boards
    D. replace lost copies

20._____

21. The *most* effective approach a station supervisor can pursue in transmitting a controversial order to his subordinates would be to state the order and

    A. briefly justify the controversial parts
    B. invite comments
    C. hold an open discussion on it
    D. explain that you expect it to be strictly obeyed

21._____

22. The *most* important reason for answering fully and completely all questions asked on accident reports is that

    A. experience has shown these questions to be necessary
    B. similar accidents will be eliminated in the future
    C. otherwise the safety committee will not be able to classify the accident
    D. it entirely eliminates the need for further investigation

22._____

23. If a station supervisor were to encounter the following conditions in the subway, the most dangerous one of them would be

    A. a flooded subway stairway as a result of heavy downpour of rain
    B. a subway car door which only opens half way at station steps
    C. crowding at the entrance to the subway escalator at the train platform level
    D. a newspaper delivery employee throwing bundles of papers off a local train at two adjacent stations

24. Assume you are preparing a report recommending a change in station cleaning procedures. It is most important that the report contain information as to

    A. when the new procedure could be put into effect
    B. whether the new procedure has already been tried
    C. the superiority of the new procedure
    D. origin of the new procedure

25. Some orders to station agents are issued orally by the station supervisor rather than by bulletin. This is because the subject matter of the verbal orders

    A. refers to less important matters
    B. is usually of local nature
    C. contains many details
    D. requires less effort to compose

26. A cleaner complains to his superior that the cleaner he relieves frequently stops to talk with passengers, and as a result, does not complete his work properly. The *most likely* conclusion would be that the porter complained of

    A. should be assigned to another location
    B. is popular with the passengers at his station
    C. is not interested in his work
    D. is lazy

27. Installation of well-designed machines capable of vending more than one fare at a time would be of greatest value to the operation of the subway system mainly because they would tend to

    A. replace railroad clerks   B. eliminate errors
    C. alleviate congestion   D. decrease necessary supervision

28. It is *most nearly* correct to say that

    A. employees who are thoroughly acquainted with the rules are most careful
    B. accidents usually result from carelessness
    C. proper supervision insures carefullness of employees
    D. a careful employee never has an accident

29. To avoid errors in station entrance computations, turnstile meters

    A. must be read at a definite time
    B. are placed on each turnstile
    C. have large and clear numbers
    D. require adequate maintenance

30. If a station agent was to see a passenger fall down a flight of stairs, his *first* action should be to

    A. request the cleaner to examine the stairs
    B. determine the cause of the accident
    C. call his office
    D. ascertain injuries

30.____

KEY (CORRECT ANSWERS)

1.	J	16.	A
2.	A	17.	B
3.	D	18.	B
4.	E	19.	C
5.	S	20.	B
6.	D	21.	A
7.	J	22.	A
8.	O	23.	D
9.	P	24.	C
10.	A	25.	B
11.	C	26.	C
12.	D	27.	C
13.	D	28.	B
14.	B	29.	A
15.	C	30.	D

EXAMINATION SECTION
TEST 1

DIRECTIONS: Each question or incomplete statement is followed by several suggested answers or completions. Select the one that BEST answers the question or completes the statement. *PRINT THE LETTER OF THE CORRECT ANSWER IN THE SPACE AT THE RIGHT.*

1. When a passenger finds a package and gives it to a cleaner, the cleaner is required to   1.____

   A. offer to escort the passenger to the nearest 24-hour booth to get a receipt
   B. take the passenger to the nearest booth so as to have a witness
   C. obtain the passenger's name and address
   D. offer to give the passenger a receipt

2. The official rules and regulations are LEAST useful in   2.____

   A. helping employees in the proper performance of their duties
   B. relieving supervisory employees of their responsibility
   C. providing a fair basis for disciplinary action
   D. encouraging safe practices

3. One of the duties of station supervisors is to   3.____

   A. check twice daily to see that railroad clerks and porters have ample supplies
   B. promptly report infractions of the rules which come to their attention
   C. be responsible for tools and equipment left by the turnstile section on stations
   D. make any changes in the station department manual of instructions that he feels are necessary

4. A passenger can request the name and pass or badge number of an employee who is in contact with the public. If this happens, the employee must provide the requested information to the passenger   4.____

   A. without delay or argument
   B. if a valid reason is given
   C. if the passenger insists strenuously
   D. without argument after first trying to placate the passenger

5. A detergent that is used in cleaning must be mixed with the correct amount of water to be effective. Assuming that the instructions state that 1 1/2 ounces of detergent should be mixed with each gallon of water, then the amount of detergent that must be used for a pail containing 2 1/2 gallons of water is closest to   5.____

   A. 37.5 ounces   B. 25 ounces
   C. 3.75 ounces   D. 2.5 ounces

6. Two walls in a station are to be cleaned. One wall is 63 feet long and 7.5 feet high, and the other wall is 46 feet long and 9 feet high.   6.____
   The *total* wall area, in square feet, to be cleaned is closest to

   A. 981   B. 886.5   C. 817.5   D. 125.5

7. Passenger trains made up of B division cars cannot be operated on A division lines MAINLY because of differences in

   A. length   B. height   C. weight   D. width

8. The result of 2/5 x 0.85 is *closest to*

   A. 3.4   B. 1.7   C. 0.34   D. 0.17

9. You have assigned two men to a job and one of the men is injured on the job. In questioning the men separately to determine the cause of the accident, you should be *mainly* interested in obtaining information pertaining to

   A. how well each man thinks the other understood your instructions
   B. the manner in which each man thinks the other performs his work
   C. what each was doing at the time the accident occurred
   D. the ability and experience of each

10. A report of an unusual occurrence is *most likely* to be accurate as to facts if written by the station supervisor

    A. *after* discussion with the station supervisor
    B. the following day, *after* thinking things over
    C. *before* discussing matters with anyone
    D. *right after* the occurrence

11. Observing an unusually large influx of passengers at one of his stations on several successive days, a station supervisor would do *best* as a FIRST step to

    A. assign several light-duty men to this station to make a traffic count
    B. contact the general manager's office to inquire as to the cause
    C. examine the area adjacent to the station to see whether there have been changes in surface transportation or housing
    D. note this fact daily on the combined railroad clerks daily fare report until a pattern has been established

12. A cleaner was injured as a result of slipping on a wet spot on a station platform. The cause of this accident would, *most likely*, be classified as due to

    A. improper apparel   B. physical condition
    C. defective equipment   D. poor housekeeping

13. Your investigation of an accident in a station would be *most fruitful* if

    A. information was obtained which might prevent similar accidents in the future
    B. the responsibility could be placed on a specific employee
    C. you found it was the fault of another department
    D. you found that the department was not responsible

14. When picking up supplies at a storeroom, a porter requests a new mop but does not have a used one to turn in.
    In this case, the *proper procedure* for the station supervisor in charge of issuing the supplies is to

    A. telephone the station department office for instructions
    B. find out what happened to the old mop
    C. issue a new mop without question
    D. deny the request

15. A cleaner does NOT sweep a certain station as often as called for on the schedule. However, when he sweeps the station, he does it thoroughly.
    In this case, it would be BEST for the station supervisor to

    A. overlook the situation
    B. insist that the cleaner follow the schedule
    C. assign the cleaner to less desirable cleaning tasks
    D. revise the cleaner's cleaning schedule the way the cleaner would like it

16. If a station supervisor observes one of his cleaners doing a cleaning job in an unsatisfactory manner, the BEST course of action for the supervisor to take is to

    A. wait until the cleaning is finished and then show the cleaner the approved method
    B. show the cleaner the approved way to do the work before allowing him to continue
    C. make a note of it and take action only if such unsatisfactory work is repeated
    D. proceed with disciplinary action and assign him to other work

17. Twelve trains, consisting of 8 cars each, arrive at a terminal station at intervals of 10 minutes. Assuming that each car carries 135 passengers, the *total* number of passengers exiting from the 12 trains is *nearest to*

    A. 16,200   B. 12,960   C. 10,800   D. 6,480

18. Six cleaners can clean a particular tile wall in 4 hours. If 3 of the cleaners leave two hours after starting work, the job would require a *total* time *closest to*

    A. 10 hours   B. 8 hours
    C. 6 hours   D. 4 hours

19. Assuming that 4 coins weigh one ounce, then 1000 coins will weigh *closest to* a total of _____ pounds.

    A. 15.6   B. 14.0   C. 12.5   D. 9.2

20. A cleaner works a regular work week of 40 hours and is paid at the rate of $14.32 per hour.
    Allowing 20% for all deductions from his gross pay, his take-home pay is *closest to*

    A. $687.36   B. $592.80   C. $458.24   D. $429.60

21. When 40% of 1,400 is subtracted from 2,100, the result is *closest to*

    A. 2,044   B. 1,700   C. 1,540   D. 1,260

22. A station supervisor is told by a train dispatcher that a certain interval is to be dropped. This means that

    A. the time interval between certain trains is to be reduced
    B. a certain train is to be taken out of service and no substitution made
    C. a certain train is to be reduced in length by a specified number of cars
    D. an additional train is to be placed in service in the interval between two regularly scheduled trains

Questions 23-26.

Questions 23 to 26 inclusive are based *solely* on the timetable on the following page. Refer to this timetable in answering these questions.

TIMETABLE - "XXX" LINE - Weekdays

	NORTHBOUND				SOUTHBOUND			
Train No.	Ave. X Leave	Ave. Y Leave	Z Road Leave	Tom Square Arrive	Tom Square Leave	Z Road Leave	Ave. Y Leave	Ave. X Arrive	X Leave
4	6:30	6:45	7:02	7:13	7:15	7:26	7:43	7:58	8:00
5	6:55	7:10	7:27	7:38	7:40	7:51	8:08	8:23	8:25
6	7:10	7:25	7:42	7:53	7:55	8:06	8:23	8:38	8:40
7	7:30	7:45	8:02	8:13	8:15	8:26	8:43	8:58	9:00
8	7:50	8:05	8:22	8:33	8:35	8:46	9:03	9:18	9:20

NOTE: Assume that arrival times at Ave. Y and Z Road are the same as the leaving times.

23. For train No. 4, the *total* layover time at Tom Square is _____ minutes.

    A. 45   B. 43   C. 3   D. 2

24. A person boarding a train at Ave. Y, desiring to arrive at Tom Square most nearly before 8:10, should take Train Number:

    A. 7   B. 6   C. 5   D. 4

25. A person entering the Ave. X station at 7:02 should arrive at Tom Square most nearly at

    A. 7:55   B. 7:53   C. 7:40   D. 7:38

26. For Train No. 8, the running time from Tom Square to Ave. X is closest to _____ minutes.

    A. 47   B. 45   C. 43   D. 41

27. In giving verbal instructions to a cleaner, the station supervisor should make them as clear and concise as possible *primarily* in order to

    A. impress the cleaner with the efficiency of transit system procedures
    B. save the cleaner's time
    C. earn the cleaner's respect
    D. avoid confusing the cleaner

28. Some of the men under your supervision present a grievance to you which you know to be common to others who report to other station supervisors.
If you feel that you have found a solution for this grievance and it appears satisfactory for your men, you *should*

    A. have the men present the solution to the superintendent through their union representative
    B. submit your solution through the Suggestion Program
    C. suggest your solution to the department through your station supervisor
    D. try out the solution on your men and, also, on men reporting to another assistant station supervisor who you know

29. A station has a total active floor area of 30,000 square feet and is to be swept three times a week.
If one cleaner can sweep 5000 sq. ft. of active area per hour, the *total* cleaner man-hours to be allotted per week for this job is closest to

    A. 24   B. 18   C. 12   D. 6

30. A storage bin for sand has inside dimensions of 6 feet long, 4 feet wide, and 3 feet high.
If the bin is full to the "2 feet" mark, the number of additional cubic feet of sand necessary to *completely* fill this bin is

    A. 48   B. 36   C. 24   D. 12

31. A station supervisor receives a telephone report from a station department employee that a stair tread is defective.
The *most important* action for the assistant supervisor to take is to

    A. see whether there are other defective treads on the stair way
    B. determine whether this defect was reported previously
    C. have the tread repaired promptly
    D. fix responsibility for the damage

32. At some stations, an additional person may be required to sell some fare cards outside a booth.
The location where this seller should stand is determined *primarily* by the

    A. line of flow of people entering the station and leaving the station
    B. number of passengers exiting the station
    C. lighting in the station
    D. number of turnstiles

33. If an employee intends to be absent from work, the book of rules and regulations requires the employee to give at least one hour notice, in person or by telephone, before the time that he is scheduled to report for duty.
The *most logical* reason for this rule is that

    A. the employee's time record can be corrected in advance
    B. a substitute can then be provided if necessary
    C. it allows time to check the employee's excuse
    D. it has a nuisance value in limiting absences

34. An employee is not permitted to give a passenger a description of any lost article which the employee has found and turned in *primarily* because

    A. this would delay the employee in his work
    B. the employee may make a mistake in the description
    C. employees are not permitted to hold conversations with passengers
    D. this might aid the passenger to claim property not belonging to him

35. The employee Suggestion Plan is beneficial *primarily* because employees

    A. have an opportunity to improve operations and receive awards
    B. acquaint themselves with the ideas of fellow employees
    C. are certain to be rewarded for making suggestions
    D. become more efficient after making suggestions

36. When checking over a particular porter's schedule for possible revisions, it is LEAST important to take into consideration whether

    A. A division or B division trains stop at the station
    B. the station involved is in a factory or residential area
    C. passengers generally traverse a large or small part of the station area
    D. passenger traffic both entering and exiting is well spread out over the day or is highly concentrated

37. You are informed unofficially by another station supervisor that one of your cleaners at a certain station is loafing on the job.
    This situation can BEST be handled by

    A. checking this cleaner's working habits yourself
    B. having the cleaner sent to your headquarters for a reprimand
    C. arranging to have the cleaner's work location changed so that he can be more readily observed
    D. ignoring the report of the other station supervisor because the cleaner is under your supervision, not his

38. The BEST assurance a station supervisor can have that a station agent knows how to do his work is if the clerk

    A. is cooperative
    B. makes few mistakes
    C. asks no questions
    D. works quickly

39. Employee morale would *most likely* be low among station personnel whose station supervisor

    A. insists on good housekeeping
    B. does not grant them special privileges
    C. does not plan the work properly
    D. enforces the rules and regulations

40. A recently appointed cleaner is assigned to duty under your supervision
 Of the following, the *most important* thing to do is to

    A. acquaint him with traffic conditions at his station
    B. make sure he knows all the rules and regulations in detail
    C. familiarize him with the schedule of working conditions for station employees
    D. take him on a tour of the station to which he will be assigned, pointing out his duties

KEY (CORRECT ANSWERS)

1. A	11. C	21. C	31. C
2. B	12. D	22. B	32. A
3. B	13. A	23. D	33. B
4. A	14. B	24. B	34. D
5. C	15. B	25. B	35. A
6. B	16. B	26. C	36. A
7. D	17. B	27. D	37. A
8. C	18. C	28. C	38. B
9. C	19. A	29. B	39. C
10. D	20. C	30. C	40. D

TEST 2

DIRECTIONS: Each question or incomplete statement is followed by several suggested answers or completions. Select the one that BEST answers the question or completes the statement. *PRINT THE LETTER OF THE CORRECT ANSWER IN THE SPACE AT THE RIGHT.*

1. You have noticed that one of the cleaners at a station in your area is frequently in the tower at the end of the platform. He tells you that he is studying for the next railroad clerk promotion examination whenever he gets a chance.
   As a station supervisor you *should*

   A. overlook this situation since it is temporary and reasonable
   B. insist that he discontinue this practice during working hours
   C. transfer the man to a station in the area without a tower
   D. inform him that he is never permitted in the tower

2. The *main* benefit to the transit system of employee training courses is that such courses

   A. tend to increase employee efficiency
   B. increase the interest of new employees
   C. prepare employees for promotion examinations
   D. are given by people well acquainted with the work

3. Of the following, the LEAST important element in good service is the

   A. cleanliness of cars and stations
   B. courtesy of the employees
   C. size of the cars
   D. relative frequency of breakdowns

4. Assume that you are appointed a station supervisor and that shortly after your appointment a more experienced station supervisor tells you that you are not making out certain reports according to standard procedures.
   In this case, you should give this criticism due consideration *primarily* because the other man

   A. has had more experience on the job
   B. is in a position to enforce his criticism
   C. will not help you in the future if his admonition is ignored
   D. is likely to report you if you do not change your procedure

5. In a report recommending a new trash handling procedure, it is *most important* that the report state

   A. whether the new procedure has already been tried
   B. the advantage or reasons for the new procedure
   C. when the new procedure will be put into effect
   D. the origin of the new procedure

6. In evaluating the services of a cleaner, a station supervisor should *primarily* consider the cleaner's

   A. readiness to report on the work of others
   B. willingness to work overtime
   C. sick leave record
   D. general dependability

7. The *most important* reason for standardizing the work procedures of railroad cleaners is that such standardization

   A. provides more of an incentive for good work
   B. enables the work to be done with less supervision
   C. prevents the porter from shirking his work
   D. encourages safe working habits

8. If a station supervisor has criticized one of his station agents for making a mistake, the station supervisor *should*

   A. give the man an opportunity to redeem himself
   B. overlook further errors which this man may make, otherwise the man may feel he is a victim of discrimination
   C. remind the man of his error from time to time in order to keep the man on his toes
   D. impress the man with the fact that all his work will be closely checked from then on

9. A station supervisor would *most likely* be at fault for inefficiency resulting from

   A. frequent labor turnover
   B. the department policy of picks
   C. improper planning of assignments
   D. delays in the delivery of material

10. Station employees should know that the third rail voltage is nearest to _____ volts.

    A. 800   B. 600   C. 240   D. 110

11. As used in the transit system, the term "collection train" applies to a

    A. work train
    B. train that is carrying passengers
    C. train that picks up refuse collected at terminals
    D. train that picks up money collected by Railroad Clerks

12. At a station located in the financial district, a station supervisor would *normally* expect the LEAST concentration of passenger traffic to occur from

    A. 5:30 P.M. to 6:30 P.M.
    B. 4:30 P.M. to 5:30 P.M.
    C. 7:30 A.M. to 8:30 A.M.
    D. 6:30 A.M. to 7:30 A.M.

13. Should it become necessary to pull an emergency alarm, the *next* move is to notify the

    A. transit police   B. power department
    C. trainmaster's office   D. track maintenance department

14. The train whistle or train horn signal that indicates that the train crew needs help is   14.____

    A. one long-one-short-one long-one short blast
    B. two long-two short blasts
    C. two long blasts
    D. one long blast

15. On a particular line, the station platforms are 600 feet in length.   15.____
    The *maximum* number of proposed new 75-foot long cars that a train on this line may have is _____ cars.

    A. 10   B. 8   C. 6   D. 4

16. If the distance between two terminals is 11.4 miles, then a train which has made 5 round trips has traveled, most nearly, _____ miles.   16.____

    A. 141   B. 114   C. 100   D. 57

17. A railroad cleaner works on the 4:00 P.M. to 12:00 Midnight shift and is paid at the hourly rate of $14.72.   17.____
    Assuming that he does not work overtime, his regular weekly pay is *closest to* :

    A. $594.20   B. $593.60   C. $592.40   D. $588.80 C

18. If 15 trains per hour are operated on a certain track, the average headway is, most nearly, _____ minutes.   18.____

    A. 6   B. 5   C. 4   D. 3

19. Employees who control the operation of signals at various points along the route of a line are called   19.____

    A. towermen   B. signal inspectors
    C. schedule makers   D. yardmasters

20. As a station supervisor, the BEST way of cooperating with your station supervisor would be to   20.____

    A. accept full responsibility for the work assigned to you
    B. make frequent suggestions for changes in work schedules
    C. continually report all details of the work under your supervision
    D. immediately report to him every infraction of the rules which you observe

21. It is *good* supervision for a station supervisor to visit his assigned stations   21.____

    A. as few times as possible
    B. on a fixed schedule only
    C. only when trouble develops
    D. at random as well as at regular intervals

22. A passenger asks you, the station supervisor, for directions how to get to a certain place on the system. If you do not know the answer, your BEST course of action is to tell the passenger

   A. to look the answer up on the map posted at the station
   B. that you do not know and try to direct him to someone who does know
   C. to get aboard the next train and to ask the conductor
   D. that only the railroad clerks are able to give such directions

23. An acquaintance who knows your position in the system complains to you that the stairway he uses to enter each morning is littered with discarded cigarette butts and wrappers, and points this out as an example of inefficiency. You know that the entrance referred to is very heavily used during the morning rush hours and that many passengers do discard cigarettes there. In the interest of good public relations, the most helpful response from you would be to

   A. point out that it is impracticable for the porter to clear the litter until after rush hour
   B. say nothing so as not to antagonize your acquaintance
   C. tell your acquaintance that you will order the porter to pay more attention
   D. suggest that your acquaintance should file a formal complaint with the transit authority

24. A station supervisor should presume that the *most likely* reason for a new worker to experience difficulty when he is learning his job is that he

   A. wants to pick it up in his own way
   B. is nervous and lacks confidence in himself
   C. has no desire to learn
   D. has no respect for his station supervisor

25. If a station agent were to see a passenger fall down a flight of stairs, his FIRST action *should be* to

   A. report the accident to his office
   B. determine the cause of the accident
   C. go to the assistance of the passenger
   D. request a porter to examine the stairs

26. For the purpose of supervision and administration, the stations are divided into a number of territorial zones.
   The *total* number of these zones is:

   A. 8   B. 6   C. 5   D. 3

27. The total number of rapid transit stations operated is, most nearly,

   A. 1,125   B. 790   C. 477   D. 214

28. The *most likely* cause of accidents involving minor injuries to trackmen is

   A. lack of safety devices
   B. careless work practices
   C. inferior equipment and materials
   D. insufficient safety posters

29. It is the primary function of tie plates to

    A. prevent the rail from creeping
    B. protect the rail against mechanical wear
    C. protect the ties against mechanical wear
    D. prevent the ties from slewing

30. It would be MOST important to question in detail a person who turns in, as found, a

    A. basket of fruit   B. five-dollar bill
    C. gold ring   D. revolver

31. A turnstile reading is 72510 at 10:00 M. and 74322 at 4:00 P.M.
    The *average* number of passengers per hour using this turnstile between the hours of 10:00 M. and 4:00 P.M. is *closest to*

    A. 703   B. 468   C. 302   D. 224

32. During a heavy snowfall, the *most practical* way for station supervisors to minimize passenger accidents at stations is to

    A. assign guards to the top and bottom of all street stairways
    B. rope off street stairways until the snowfall stops
    C. keep cleaners on snow duty until street stairways are clear
    D. post signs at street entrances warning passengers to be careful

33. Cleaners' instructions state that cloths which have been used for applying lemon oil should be kept in a metal container.
    The *most important* reason for this instruction is that exposed oily cloths

    A. have a bad odor
    B. collect dirt
    C. breed germs
    D. are a fire hazard

34. A cleaner works the following schedule during a certain week: Monday, 4:00 P.M. to 12 Midnight; Tuesday, 4:00 P.M. to 1:00 A.M.; Wednesday, 4:00 P.M. to 8:00 A.M.; Thursday, 4:00 P.M. to 12 Midnight; and Friday, 4:00 P.M. to 4:00 A.M.
    The *total* time in hours that the porter worked during this week is *closest to*

    A. 79   B. 59.5   C. 53   D. 40

35. Block tickets issued by station agents

    A. can be presented for free rides within a week of the day that they were issued
    B. must be packaged in lots of 100 at the end of each tour
    C. may be redeemed for cash at the request of passengers
    D. represent free rides given to compensate for incomplete rides

36. Area control booths are NOT used as

    A. storage points for station department forms
    B. mail delivery and pick-up points
    C. reporting points for night lunch reliefs
    D. lost property receiving points

37. According to the book of rules and regulations, employees may engage in card playing while on system property

   A. at no time
   B. just before or after working hours
   C. when not actively performing their duties
   D. only during the lunch period

38. The specific amount of money in the change fund allocated to a booth may be increased by a railroad clerk upon proper authorization and by making proper notation in his daily fare report *and*

   A. adjusting the bagging of receipts
   B. transferring the authorized amount from another booth
   C. borrowing the authorized increase from his personal funds
   D. obtaining an allotment of the additional amount from the revenue department

39. A station agent on duty in the subway need NOT make a report

   A. of water leaking through the subway ceiling
   B. if a passenger tore his clothing on a protruding nail
   C. of a passenger who is dissatisfied with the schedule
   D. if he is told that a passenger tripped on the stairs and was injured

40. Station supervisors on the 4 P.M. to midnight trick are responsible for the

   A. collection of all torn and dirty revenue bags
   B. storing all special work train deliveries, such as sawdust
   C. ordering and distributing the cleaning supplies for cleaners
   D. ordering and control of all stationery supplies used by railroad clerks

KEY (CORRECT ANSWERS)

1. B	11. D	21. D	31. C
2. A	12. D	22. B	32. C
3. C	13. C	23. A	33. D
4. A	14. A	24. B	34. C
5. B	15. B	25. C	35. D
6. D	16. B	26. A	36. A
7. B	17. D	27. B	37. A
8. A	18. C	28. B	38. A
9. C	19. A	29. C	39. C
10. B	20. A	30. D	40. D

READING COMPREHENSION
UNDERSTANDING AND INTERPRETING WRITTEN MATERIAL
EXAMINATION SECTION
TEST 1

DIRECTIONS: Each question or incomplete statement is followed by several suggested answers or completions. Select the one that BEST answers the question or completes the statement. *PRINT THE LETTER OF THE CORRECT ANSWER IN THE SPACE AT THE RIGHT.*

Questions 1-8.

DIRECTIONS: Questions 1 through 8 are to be answered on the basis of the following regulations governing Newspaper Carriers when on subway trains or station platforms. These Newspaper Carriers are issued badges which entitle them to enter subway stations, when carrying papers in accordance with these regulations, without paying a fare.

REGULATIONS GOVERNING NEWSPAPER CARRIERS WHEN ON SUBWAY TRAINS OR STATION PLATFORMS

1. Carriers must wear badges at all times when on trains.
2. Carriers must not sort, separate, or wrap bundles on trains or insert sections.
3. Carriers must not obstruct platform of cars or stations.
4. Carriers may make delivery to stands inside the stations by depositing their badge with the station agent.
5. Throwing of bundles is strictly prohibited and will be cause for arrest.
6. Each bundle must not be over 18" x 12" x 15".
7. Not more than two bundles shall be carried by each carrier. (An extra fare to be charged for a second bundle.)
8. No wire to be used on bundles carried into stations.

1. These regulations do NOT prohibit carriers on trains from _____ newspapers. 1.____

    A. sorting bundles of
    B. carrying bundles of
    C. wrapping bundles of
    D. inserting sections into

2. A carrier delivering newspapers to a stand inside of the station MUST 2.____

    A. wear his badge at all times
    B. leave his badge with the railroad clerk
    C. show his badge to the railroad clerk
    D. show his badge at the newsstand

3. Carriers are warned against throwing bundles of newspapers from trains MAINLY because these acts may 3.____

    A. wreck the stand
    B. cause injury to passengers
    C. hurt the carrier
    D. damage the newspaper

4. It is permissible for a carrier to temporarily leave his bundles of newspapers

   A. near the subway car's door
   B. at the foot of the station stairs
   C. in front of the exit gate
   D. on a station bench

4.____

5. Of the following, the carrier who should NOT be restricted from entering the subway is the one carrying a bundle which is _____ long, _____ wide, and _____ high.

   A. 15"; 18"; 18"
   B. 18"; 12"; 18"
   C. 18"; 12"; 15"
   D. 18"; 15"; 15"

5.____

6. A carrier who will have to pay one fare is carrying _____ bundle(s).

   A. one   B. two   C. three   D. four

6.____

7. Wire may NOT be used for tying bundles because it may be

   A. rusty
   B. expensive
   C. needed for other purposes
   D. dangerous to other passengers

7.____

8. If a carrier is arrested in violation of these regulations, the PROBABLE reason is that he

   A. carried too many papers
   B. was not wearing his badge
   C. separated bundles of newspapers on the train
   D. tossed a bundle of newspapers to a carrier on a train

8.____

Questions 9-12.

DIRECTIONS: Questions 9 through 12 are to be answered on the basis of the Bulletin printed below. Read this Bulletin carefully before answering these questions. Select your answers ONLY on the basis of this Bulletin.

BULLETIN

Rule 107(m) states, in part, that *Before closing doors they (Conductors) must afford passengers an opportunity to detrain and entrain...*

Doors must be left open long enough to allow passengers to enter and exit from the train. Closing doors on passengers too quickly does not help to shorten the station stop and is a violation of the safety and courtesy which must be accorded to all our passengers.

The proper and effective way to keep passengers moving in and out of the train is to use the public address system. When the train is excessively crowded and passengers on the platform are pushing those in the cars, it may be necessary to close the doors after a reasonable period of time has been allowed.

Closing doors on passengers too quickly is a violation of rules and will be cause for disciplinary actions.

9. Which of the following statements is CORRECT about closing doors on passengers too quickly? It

   A. will shorten the running time from terminal to terminal
   B. shortens the station stop but is a violation of safety and courtesy
   C. does not help shorten the station stop time
   D. makes the passengers detrain and entrain quicker

10. The BEST way to get passengers to move in and out of cars quickly is to

    A. have the platform conductors urge passengers to move into doorways
    B. make announcements over the public address system
    C. start closing doors while passengers are getting on
    D. set a fixed time for stopping at each station

11. The conductor should leave doors open at each station stop long enough for passengers to

    A. squeeze into an excessively crowded train
    B. get from the local to the express train
    C. get off and get on the train
    D. hear the announcements over the public address system

12. Closing doors on passengers too quickly is a violation of rules and is cause for

    A. the conductor's immediate suspension
    B. the conductor to be sent back to the terminal for another assignment
    C. removal of the conductor at the next station
    D. disciplinary action to be taken against the conductor

Questions 13-15.

DIRECTIONS: Questions 13 through 15 are to be answered on the basis of the Bulletin printed below. Read this Bulletin carefully before answering these questions. Select your answers ONLY on the basis of this Bulletin.

BULLETIN

Conductors assigned to train service are not required to wear uniform caps from June 1 to September 30, inclusive.

Conductors assigned to platform duty are required to wear the uniform cap at all times. Conductors are reminded that they must furnish their badge numbers to anyone who requests same.

During the above-mentioned period, conductors may remove their uniform coats. The regulation summer short-sleeved shirts must be worn with the regulation uniform trousers. Suspenders are not permitted if the uniform coat is removed. Shoes are to be black but sandals, sneakers, suede, canvas, or two-tone footwear must not be worn.

Conductors may work without uniform tie if the uniform coat is removed. However, only the top collar button may be opened. The tie may not be removed if the uniform coat is worn.

13. Conductors assigned to platform duty are required to wear uniform caps

    A. at all times except from June 1 to September 30, inclusive
    B. whenever they are on duty
    C. only from June 1 to September 30, inclusive
    D. only when they remove their uniform coats

14. Suspenders are permitted ONLY if conductors wear

    A. summer short-sleeved shirts with uniform trousers
    B. uniform trousers without belt loops
    C. the type permitted by the authority
    D. uniform coats

15. A conductor MUST furnish his badge number to

    A. authority supervisors only
    B. members of special inspection only
    C. anyone who asks him for it
    D. passengers only

Questions 16-17.

DIRECTIONS: Questions 16 and 17 are to be answered SOLELY on the basis of the following Bulletin.

BULLETIN

Effective immediately, Conductors on trains equipped with public address systems shall make the following announcements in addition to their regular station announcement. At stations where passengers normally board trains from their homes or places of employment, the announcement shall be *Good Morning* or *Good Afternoon* or *Good Evening,* depending on the time of the day. At stations where passengers normally leave trains for their homes or places of employment, the announcement shall be *Have a Good Day* or *Good Night,* depending on the time of day or night.

16. The MAIN purpose of making the additional announcements mentioned in the Bulletin is MOST likely to

    A. keep passengers informed about the time of day
    B. determine whether the public address system works in case of an emergency
    C. make the passengers' ride more pleasant
    D. have the conductor get used to using the public address system

17. According to this Bulletin, a conductor should greet passengers boarding the *D* train at the Coney Island Station at 8 A.M. Monday by announcing

    A. Have a Good Day
    B. Good Morning
    C. Watch your step as you leave
    D. Good Evening

Questions 18-25.

DIRECTIONS: Questions 18 through 25 are to be answered on the basis of the information regarding the incident given below. Read this information carefully before answering these questions.

INCIDENT

As John Brown, a cleaner, was sweeping the subway station platform, in accordance with his assigned schedule, he was accused by Henry Adams of unnecessarily bumping him with the broom and scolded for doing this work when so many passengers were on the platform. Adams obtained Brown's badge number and stated that he would report the matter to the Transit Authority. Standing around and watching this were Mary Smith, a schoolteacher, Ann Jones, a student, and Joe Black, a maintainer, with Jim Roe, his helper, who had been working on one of the turnstiles. Brown thereupon proceeded to take the names and addresses of these people as required by the Transit Authority rule which directs that names and addresses of as many disinterested witnesses be taken as possible. Shortly thereafter, a train arrived at the station and Adams, as well as several other people, boarded the train and left. Brown went back to his work of sweeping the station.

18. The cleaner was sweeping the station at this time because

    A. the platform was unusually dirty
    B. there were very few passengers on the platform
    C. he had no regard for the passengers
    D. it was set by his work schedule

19. This incident proves that

    A. witnesses are needed in such cases
    B. porters are generally careless
    C. subway employees stick together
    D. brooms are dangerous in the subway

20. Joe Black was a

    A. helper   B. maintainer
    C. cleaner   D. teacher

21. The number of persons witnessing this incident was

    A. 2   B. 3   C. 4   D. 5

22. The addresses of witnesses are required so that they may later be

    A. depended on to testify   B. recognized
    C. paid   D. located

23. The person who said he would report this incident to the transit authority was

    A. Black   B. Adams   C. Brown   D. Roe

24. The ONLY person of the following who positively did NOT board the train was

  A. Brown B. Smith C. Adams D. Jones

25. As a result of this incident,
  A. no action need be taken against the cleaner unless Adams makes a written complaint
  B. the cleaner should be given the rest of the day off
  C. the handles of the brooms used should be made shorter
  D. Brown's badge number should be changed

KEY (CORRECT ANSWERS)

1. B
2. B
3. B
4. D
5. C

6. A
7. D
8. D
9. C
10. B

11. C
12. D
13. B
14. D
15. C

16. C
17. B
18. D
19. A
20. B

21. C
22. D
23. B
24. A
25. A

TEST 2

DIRECTIONS: Each question or incomplete statement is followed by several suggested answers or completions. Select the one that BEST answers the question or completes the statement. *PRINT THE LETTER OF THE CORRECT ANSWER IN THE SPACE AT THE RIGHT.*

Questions 1-10.

DIRECTIONS: Questions 1 through 10 are to be answered on the basis of the information contained in the following safety rules. Read the rules carefully before answering these questions.

SAFETY RULES

Employees must take every precaution to prevent accidents, or injury to persons, or damage to property. For this reason, they must observe conditions of the equipment and tools with which they work, and the structures upon which they work.

It is the duty of all employees to report to their superior all dangerous conditions which they may observe. Employees must use every precaution to prevent the origin of fire. If they discover smoke or a fire in the subway, they shall proceed to the nearest telephone and notify the trainmaster giving their name, badge number, and location of the trouble.

In case of accidents on the subway system, employees must, if possible, secure the name, address, and telephone number of any passengers who may have been injured.

Employees at or near the location of trouble on the subway system, whether it be a fire or an accident, shall render all practical assistance which they are qualified to perform.

1. The BEST way for employees to prevent an accident is to
    A. secure the names of the injured persons
    B. arrive promptly at the location of the accident
    C. give their name and badge numbers to the trainmaster
    D. take all necessary precautions

2. In case of trouble, trackmen are NOT expected to
    A. report fires
    B. give help if they don't know how
    C. secure telephone numbers of persons injured in subway accidents
    D. give their badge number to anyone

3. Trackmen MUST
    A. be present at all fires
    B. see all accidents
    C. report dangerous conditions
    D. be the first to discover smoke in the subway

4. Observing conditions means to 4.____

 A. look at things carefully
 B. report what you see
 C. ignore things that are none of your business
 D. correct dangerous conditions

5. A dangerous condition existing on the subway system which a trackman should observe and report to his superior would be 5.____

 A. passengers crowding into trains
 B. trains running behind schedule
 C. tools in defective condition
 D. some newspapers on the track

6. If a trackman discovers a badly worn rail, he should 6.____

 A. not take any action
 B. remove the worn section of rail
 C. notify his superior
 D. replace the rail

7. The MAIN reason a trackman should observe the condition of his tools is 7.____

 A. so that they won't be stolen
 B. because they don't belong to him
 C. to prevent accidents
 D. because they cannot be replaced

8. If a passenger who paid his fare is injured in a subway accident, it is MOST important that an employee obtain the passenger's 8.____

 A. name
 C. badge number
 B. age
 D. destination

9. An employee who happens to be at the scene of an accident on a crowded station of the system should 9.____

 A. not give assistance unless he chooses to do so
 B. leave the scene immediately
 C. question all bystanders
 D. render whatever assistance he can

10. If a trackman discovers a fire at one end of a station platform and telephones the information to the trainmaster, he need NOT give 10.____

 A. the trainmaster's name
 B. the name of the station involved
 C. his own name
 D. the number of his badge

Questions 11-15.

DIRECTIONS: Questions 11 through 15 are to be answered on the basis of the information contained in the safety regulations given below. Refer to these rules in answering these questions.

REGULATIONS FOR SMALL GROUPS WHO MOVE FROM POINT TO POINT ON THE TRACKS

Employees who perform duties on the tracks in small groups and who move from point to point along the trainway must be on the alert at all times and prepared to clear the track when a train approaches without unnecessarily slowing it down. Underground at all times, and out-of-doors between sunset and sunrise, such employees must not enter upon the tracks unless each of them is equipped with an approved light. Flashlights must not be used for protection by such groups. Upon clearing the track to permit a train to pass, each member of the group must give a proceed signal, by hand or light, to the motorman of the train. Whenever such small groups are working in an area protected by caution lights or flags, but are not members of the gang for whom the flagging protection was established, they must not give proceed signals to motormen. The purpose of this rule is to avoid a motorman's confusing such signal with that of the flagman who is protecting a gang. Whenever a small group is engaged in work of an engrossing nature or at any time when the view of approaching trains is limited by reason of curves or otherwise, one man of the group, equipped with a whistle, must be assigned properly to warn and protect the man or men at work and must not perform any other duties while so assigned.

11. If a small group of men are traveling along the tracks toward their work location and a train approaches, they should

    A. stop the train
    B. signal the motorman to go slowly
    C. clear the track
    D. stop immediately

12. Small groups may enter upon the tracks

    A. only between sunset and sunrise
    B. provided each has an approved light
    C. provided their foreman has a good flashlight
    D. provided each man has an approved flashlight

13. After a small group has cleared the tracks in an area unprotected by caution lights or flags,

    A. each member must give the proceed signal to the motorman
    B. the foreman signals the motorman to proceed
    C. the motorman can proceed provided he goes slowly
    D. the last member off the tracks gives the signal to the motorman

14. If a small group is working in an area protected by the signals of a track gang, the members of the small group

    A. need not be concerned with train movement
    B. must give the proceed signal together with the track gang

C. can delegate one of their members to give the proceed signal
D. must not give the proceed signal

15. If the view of approaching trains is blocked, the small group should

    A. move to where they can see the trains
    B. delegate one of the group to warn and protect them
    C. keep their ears alert for approaching trains
    D. refuse to work at such locations

15.____

Questions 16-25.

DIRECTIONS: Questions 16 through 25 are to be answered SOLELY on the basis of the article about general safety precautions given below.

GENERAL SAFETY PRECAUTIONS

When work is being done on or next to a track on which regular trains are running, special signals must be displayed as called for in the general rules for flagging. Yellow caution signals, green clear signals, and a flagman with a red danger signal are required for the protection of traffic and workmen in accordance with the standard flagging rules. The flagman shall also carry a white signal for display to the motorman when he may proceed. The foreman in charge must see that proper signals are displayed.

On elevated lines during daylight hours, the yellow signal shall be a yellow flag, the red signal shall be a red flag, the green signal shall be a green flag, and the white signal shall be a white flag. In subway sections, and on elevated lines after dark, the yellow signal shall be a yellow lantern, the red signal shall be a red lantern, the green signal shall be a green lantern, and the white signal shall be a white lantern.

Caution and clear signals are to be secured to the elevated or subway structure with non-metallic fastenings outside the clearance line of the train and on the motorman's side of the track.

16. On elevated lines during daylight hours, the caution signal is a

    A. yellow lantern   B. green lantern
    C. yellow flag   D. green flag

16.____

17. In subway sections, the clear signal is a

    A. yellow lantern   B. green lantern
    C. yellow flag   D. green flag

17.____

18. The MINIMUM number of lanterns that a subway track flagman should carry is

    A. 1   B. 2   C. 3   D. 4

18.____

19. The PRIMARY purpose of flagging is to protect the

    A. flagman   B. motorman
    C. track workers   D. railroad

19.____

20. A suitable fastening for securing caution lights to the elevated or subway structure is   20.____

    A. copper nails   B. steel wire
    C. brass rods   D. cotton twine

21. On elevated structures during daylight hours, the red flag is held by the   21.____

    A. motorman   B. foreman   C. trackman   D. flagman

22. The signal used in the subway to notify a motorman to proceed is a   22.____

    A. white lantern   B. green lantern
    C. red flag   D. yellow flag

23. The caution, clear, and danger signals are displayed for the information of   23.____

    A. trackmen   B. workmen   C. flagmen   D. motormen

24. Since the motorman's cab is on the right-hand side, caution signals should be secured to the   24.____

    A. right-hand running rail
    B. left-hand running rail
    C. structure to the right of the track
    D. structure to the left of the track

25. In a track work gang, the person responsible for the proper display of signals is the   25.____

    A. track worker   B. foreman
    C. motorman   D. flagman

KEY (CORRECT ANSWERS)

1. D	11. C
2. B	12. B
3. C	13. A
4. A	14. D
5. C	15. B
6. C	16. C
7. C	17. B
8. A	18. B
9. D	19. C
10. A	20. D

21. D
22. A
23. D
24. C
25. B

TEST 3

DIRECTIONS: Each question or incomplete statement is followed by several suggested answers or completions. Select the one that BEST answers the question or completes the statement. *PRINT THE LETTER OF THE CORRECT ANSWER IN THE SPACE AT THE RIGHT.*

Questions 1-6.

DIRECTIONS: Questions 1 through 6 are to be answered on the basis of the Bulletin Order given below. Refer to this bulletin when answering these questions.

<u>BULLETIN ORDER NO. 67</u>

SUBJECT: Procedure for Handling Fire Occurrences

In order that the Fire Department may be notified of all fires, even those that have been extinguished by our own employees, any employee having knowledge of a fire must notify the Station Department Office immediately on telephone extensions D-4177, D-4181, D-4185, or D-4189.

Specific information regarding the fire should include the location of the fire, the approximate distance north or south of the nearest station, and the track designation, line, and division.

In addition, the report should contain information as to the status of the fire and whether our forces have extinguished it or if Fire Department equipment is required.

When all information has been obtained, the Station Supervisor in Charge in the Station Department Office will notify the Desk Trainmaster of the Division involved.

Richard Roe,
Superintendent

1. An employee having knowledge of a fire should FIRST notify the

   A. Station Department Office
   B. Fire Department
   C. Desk Trainmaster
   D. Station Supervisor

2. If bulletin order number 1 was issued on January 2, bulletins are being issued at the monthly average of

   A. 8   B. 10   C. 12   D. 14

3. It is clear from the bulletin that

   A. employees are expected to be expert fire fighters
   B. many fires occur on the transit system
   C. train service is usually suspended whenever a fire occurs
   D. some fires are extinguished without the help of the Fire Department

4. From the information furnished in this bulletin, it can be assumed that the

   A. Station Department office handles a considerable number of telephone calls
   B. Superintendent Investigates the handling of all subway fires
   C. Fire Department is notified only in ease of large fires
   D. employee first having knowledge of the fire must call all 4 extensions

5. The PROBABLE reason for notifying the Fire Department even when the fire has been extinguished by a subway employee is because the Fire Department is

   A. a city agency
   B. still responsible to check the fire
   C. concerned with fire prevention
   D. required to clean up after the fire

6. Information about the fire NOT specifically required is

   A. track   B. time of day   C. station   D. division

Questions 7-10.

DIRECTIONS: Questions 7 through 10 are to be answered on the basis of the paragraph on fire fighting shown below. When answering these questions, refer to this paragraph.

FIRE FIGHTING

A security officer should remember the cardinal rule that water or soda acid fire extinguishers should not be used on any electrical fire, and apply it in the case of a fire near the third rail. In addition, security officers should familiarize themselves with all available fire alarms and fire-fighting equipment within their assigned posts. Use of the fire alarm should bring responding Fire Department apparatus quickly to the scene. Familiarity with the fire-fighting equipment near his post would help in putting out incipient fires. Any man calling for the Fire Department should remain outside so that he can direct the Fire Department to the fire. As soon as possible thereafter, the special inspection desk must be notified, and a complete written report of the fire, no matter how small, must be submitted to this office. The security officer must give the exact time and place it started, who discovered it, how it was extinguished, the damage done, cause of same, list of any injured persons with the extent of their injuries, and the name of the Fire Chief in charge. All defects noticed by the security officer concerning the fire alarm or any fire-fighting equipment must be reported to the special inspection department.

7. It would be PROPER to use water to put out a fire in a(n)

   A. electric motor   B. electric switch box
   C. waste paper trash can   D. electric generator

8. After calling the Fire Department from a street box to report a fire, the security officer should then

   A. return to the fire and help put it out
   B. stay outside and direct the Fire Department to the fire
   C. find a phone and call his boss
   D. write out a report for the special inspection desk

9. A security officer is required to submit a complete written report of a fire　　　　9._____

   A. two weeks after the fire
   B. the day following the fire
   C. as soon as possible
   D. at his convenience

10. In his report of a fire, it is NOT necessary for the security officer to state　　　　10._____

    A. time and place of the fire
    B. who discovered the fire
    C. the names of persons injured
    D. quantity of Fire Department equipment used

Questions 11-16.

DIRECTIONS:　Questions 11 through 16 are to be answered on the basis of the Notice given below. Refer to this Notice in answering these questions.

NOTICE

Your attention is called to Route Request Buttons that are installed on all new type Interlocking Home Signals where there is a choice of route in the midtown area. The route request button is to be operated by the motorman when the home signal is at danger and no call-on is displayed or when improper route is displayed.

To operate, the motorman will press the button for the desiredroute as indicated under each button; a light will then go on over the buttons to inform the motorman that his request has been registered in the tower.

If the towerman desires to give the motorman a route other than the one he selected, the towerman will cancel out the light over the route selection buttons. The motorman will then accept the route given.

If no route or call-on is given, the motorman will sound his whistle for the signal maintainer, secure his train, and call the desk trainmaster.

11. The official titles of the two classes of employee whose actions would MOST frequently be affected by the contents of this notice are　　　　11._____

    A. motorman and trainmaster
    B. signal maintainer and trainmaster
    C. towerman and motorman
    D. signal maintainer and towerman

12. A motorman should use a route request button when　　　　12._____

    A. the signal indicates proceed on main line
    B. a call-on is displayed
    C. the signal indicates stop
    D. the signal indicates proceed on diverging route

13. The PROPER way to request a route is to   13.____

    A. press the button corresponding to the desired route
    B. press the button a number of times to correspond with the number of the route requested
    C. stop at the signal and blow four short blasts
    D. stop at the signal and telephone the tower

14. The motorman will know that his requested route has been registered in the tower if   14.____

    A. a light comes on over the route request buttons
    B. an acknowledging signal is sounded on the tower horn
    C. the light in the route request button goes dark
    D. the home signal continues to indicate stop

15. Under certain conditions, when stopped at such home signal, the motorman must signal for a signal maintainer and call the desk trainmaster.   15.____
    Such condition exists when, after standing awhile,

    A. the towerman continues to give the wrong route
    B. the towerman does not acknowledge the signal
    C. no route or call-on is given
    D. the light over the route request buttons is cancelled out

16. It is clear that route request buttons   16.____

    A. eliminate train delays due to signals at junctions
    B. keep the towerman alert
    C. force motormen and towermen to be more careful
    D. are a more accurate form of communication than the whistle.

Questions 17-22.

DIRECTIONS: Questions 17 through 22 are to be answered on the basis of the instructions for removal of paper given below. Read these instructions carefully before answering these questions.

GENERAL INSTRUCTIONS FOR REMOVAL OF PAPER

When a cleaner's work schedule calls for the bagging of paper, he will remove paper from the waste paper receptacles, bag it, and place the bags at the head end of the platform, where they will be picked up by the work train. He will fill bags with paper to a weight that can be carried without danger of personal injury, as porters are forbidden to drag bags of paper over the platform. Cleaners are responsible that all bags of paper are arranged so as to prevent their falling from the platform to tracks, and so as to not interfere with passenger traffic.

17. A GOOD reason for removing the paper from receptacles and placing it in bags is that bags are more easily   17.____

    A. stored   B. weighed   C. handled   D. emptied

18. The *head end* of a local station platform is the end   18.____

    A. in the direction that trains are running
    B. nearest to which the trains stop
    C. where there is an underpass to the other side
    D. at which the change booth is located

19. The MOST likely reason for having the filled bags placed at the head end of the station rather than at the other end is that   19.____

    A. a special storage space is provided there for them
    B. this end of the platform is farthest from the passengers
    C. most porters' closets are located near the head end
    D. the work train stops at this end to pick them up

20. Limiting the weight to which the bags can be filled is PROBABLY done to   20.____

    A. avoid having too many ripped or broken bags
    B. protect the porter against possible rupture
    C. make sure that all bags are filled fairly evenly
    D. insure that, when stored, the bags will not fall to the track

21. The MOST important reason for not allowing filled bags to be dragged over the platform is that the bags   21.____

    A. could otherwise be loaded too heavily
    B. might leave streaks on the platform
    C. would wear out too quickly
    D. might spill paper on the platform

22. The instructions do NOT hold a porter responsible for a bag of paper which   22.____

    A. is torn due to dragging over a platform
    B. falls on a passenger because it was poorly stacked
    C. falls to the track without being pushed
    D. is ripped open by school children

Questions 23-25.

DIRECTIONS: Questions 23 through 25 are to be answered on the basis of the situation described below. Consider the facts given in this situation when answering these questions.

SITUATION

A new detergent that is to be added to water and the resulting mixture just wiped on any surface has been tested by the station department and appeared to be excellent. However, you notice, after inspecting a large number of stations that your porters have cleaned with this detergent, that the surfaces cleaned are not as clean as they formerly were when the old method was used.

23. The MAIN reason for the station department testing the new detergent in the first place was to make certain that 23.____

    A. it was very simple to use
    B. a little bit would go a long way
    C. there was no stronger detergent on the market
    D. it was superior to anything formerly used

24. The MAIN reason that such a poor cleaning job resulted was MOST likely due to the 24.____

    A. porters being lax on the job
    B. detergent not being as good as expected
    C. incorrect amount of water being mixed with the detergent
    D. fact that the surfaces cleaned needed to be scrubbed

25. The reason for inspecting a number of stations was to 25.____

    A. determine whether all porters did the same job
    B. insure that the result of the cleaning job was the same in each location
    C. be certain that the detergent was used in each station inspected
    D. see whether certain surfaces cleaned better than others

KEY (CORRECT ANSWERS)

1. A		11. C	
2. C		12. C	
3. D		13. A	
4. A		14. A	
5. C		15. C	
6. B		16. D	
7. C		17. C	
8. B		18. A	
9. C		19. D	
10. D		20. B	

21. C
22. D
23. D
24. B
25. B

ARITHMETICAL REASONING

EXAMINATION SECTION
TEST 1

DIRECTIONS: Each question or incomplete statement is followed by several suggested answers or completions. Select the one that BEST answers the question or completes the statement. *PRINT THE LETTER OF THE CORRECT ANSWER IN THE SPACE AT THE RIGHT.*

1. The distance covered in four minutes by a subway train traveling at 30 mph is _____ mile(s).
    A. 1   B. 1 1/2   C. 2   D. 3

2. The jaws of a vise close 3/16" for each turn of the screw. If the vise is open 6 inches, the number of turns to close the jaws completely is
    A. 29   B. 30   C. 31   D. 32

3. The sum of 3"2 1/4", 0'8 7/8", 2'9 3/4", and 1'0" is
    A. 7'8 7/8"   B. 7'9"
    C. 8'0 7/8"   D. 15'0 7/8"

4. It was estimated that a certain track concreting job would require 40 cubic yards of concrete. Actually, the job took 38 1/2 cubic yards.
   The percentage error from the estimate is MOST NEARLY
    A. 2%   B. 4%   C. 6%   D. 8%

5. A 39-foot length of running rail weighing 100 lbs. per yard has a total weight of _____ lbs.
    A. 390   B. 780   C. 1,300   D. 3,900

6. The pay of a trackman for a 40-hour week at $19.39 an hour is
    A. $775.60   B. $738.60   C. $777.60   D. $789.60

7. If a train on a certain route makes two roundtrips in 5 hours and 20 minutes, the average time for one roundtrip would be _____ hour(s) _____ minutes.
    A. 1; 20   B. 2; 30   C. 2; 40   D. 3; 10

8. It is estimated that it will take 6 men working for 6 days to complete a certain track maintenance job.
   If, when the job is started, only 4 men can be made available, you can estimate that the number of days needed for these men to complete the job will be
    A. 4   B. 6   C. 9   D. 13 1/2

9. A certain track job, which takes 3 days to complete, requires 7 trackmen at $16.245 per hour and a gang foreman whose annual salary is equivalent to $138.60 per day.
   The TOTAL labor cost for the job is (assuming an 8-hr. work day)
    A. $756.91   B. $1,325.52   C. $3,144.96   D. $8,671.20

10. A certain track job, which took 4 days to complete, required 6 trackmen at $15.15 per hour and a gang foreman whose annual salary is equivalent to $128.00 per day. The TOTAL labor cost for the job was

   A. $855.20   B. $875.60   C. $1,239.20   D. $3,420.80

11. The sum of the fractions 5/16, 5/8, and 21/32 is MOST NEARLY

   A. 1.491   B. 1.594   C. 1.630   D. 1.642

12. If a maintainer earns $10.82 per hour and time and one-half for overtime, his gross salary for a week in which he works 2 hours over his regular 40 hours should be

   A. $433.60   B. $449.86   C. $455.28   D. $465.26

13. It is common knowledge among railroad men that a speed of 15 miles per hour is exactly equal to 22 feet per second.
    In accordance with this rule, select the FASTEST of the following speeds:

   A. 70 feet per second
   B. 50 miles per hour
   C. 0.9 mile per minute
   D. 4,500 feet per minute

14. Several months ago, the rush hour headway on the Rockaway Line was increased from 16 minutes to 24 minutes.
    This represents a reduction in train service of APPROXIMATELY (SEE NOTE BELOW)

   A. 25%   B. 33%   C. 50%   D. 67%

15. The running time between two local terminals is 40 minutes. If the average speed of the trains on this run is 15 mph, the distance between these terminals is APPROXIMATELY _____ miles.

   A. 8   B. 10   C. 12   D. 14

16. A ten-car train took 6 minutes to travel between two stations which are 3 miles apart. The average speed of the train was _____ mph.

   A. 20   B. 25   C. 30   D. 35

17. Trains on a certain track operate on a 2-minute headway at a speed of 30 miles per hour. A CORRECT expression for calculating the number of feet of distance between the front of one train and the front of the train ahead when both trains are running at the given speed is

   A. 30/60 x 2 x 5,280
   B. 2/30 x 60 x 5,280
   C. 30/60 x 1/2 x 5,280
   D. 30/2 x 1/60 x 5,280

   NOTE: Assume headway is calculated by dividing the total number of cars by the time, in minutes, required to pass a particular point.

18. Motormen are permitted to *economize* on time when it can be done safely after a delay. In order to save one minute on a one-mile stretch for which the timetable schedules an average speed of 15 miles per hour, the motormen would have to average _____ mph.

   A. 17   B. 20   C. 22   D. 25

19. If the distance between two terminals is 8.3 miles, then a train which made 6 roundtrips traveled about _____ miles.

    A. 50　　　　B. 65　　　　C. 85　　　　D. 100

20. A certain subway line has been extended to include five more local stations. Assuming that the schedule time for each local run averages 1 1/2 minutes, the number of minutes that should be added to the scheduled roundtrip time due to this extension is NEAREST to _____ minutes.

    A. 7 1/2　　　B. 10　　　　C. 12 1/2　　　D. 15

21. The first of three storage tracks holds as many cars as the other two together, and the second holds twice as many cars as the third.
    If the first track holds 30 cars, the first and third tracks together hold _____ cars.

    A. 60　　　　B. 50　　　　C. 45　　　　D. 40

22. In a four-track lay-up yard, there are 3 cars on each of two tracks and 6 cars on each of the other two tracks. If each lay-up track can hold 10 cars, the MINIMUM number of train movements required to set up a ten-car train on one of the lay-up tracks is

    A. 2　　　　B. 3　　　　C. 4　　　　D. 5

23. The service on a certain four-track line consists of 24 trains per hour on each express track and 21 trains per hour on each local track. Assume there are 2 locals & 2 express tracks. The TOTAL number of all trains passing a given point on this line in any 10-minute period is

    A. 7　　　　B. 9　　　　C. 15　　　　D. 45

24. An express train requires five minutes to make the run between two stations which are two miles apart.
    The AVERAGE speed of the train, in miles per hour, for this run is

    A. 15　　　　B. 20　　　　C. 24　　　　D. 30

25. A road motorman, paid $13.40 an hour, reports for work on Wednesday at 7:30 A.M. and normally clears at 3:00 P.M.
    What is his gross pay for the day if he is required to take 1 hr. to write an unusual occurrence report at the end of this run?

    A. $105.20　　B. $107.20　　C. $113.90　　D. $120.60

KEY (CORRECT ANSWERS)

1.	C	11.	B
2.	D	12.	D
3.	A	13.	C
4.	B	14.	B
5.	C	15.	B
6.	A	16.	C
7.	C	17.	A
8.	C	18.	B
9.	C	19.	D
10.	D	20.	D

21. D
22. A
23. C
24. C
25. C

SOLUTIONS TO PROBLEMS

1. Let x = distance in miles. Then, $30/60 = x/4$. Solving, $x = 2$

2. Number of turns = $6 \div \dfrac{3}{16} = 32$

3. 3' 2 1/4" + 0' 8 7/8" + 2' 9 3/4" + 1' 0" = 6' 20 7/8" = 7' 8 7/8"

4. $(40 - 38\ 1/2) \div 40 = 3.75\% \approx 4\%$

5. $(100)(39/3) = 1300$ lbs.

6. $(\$19.39)(40) = \$775.60$

7. (5 hrs. 20 min.) ÷ 2 = 320 min. ÷ 2 = 160 min. = 2 hrs. 40 min.

8. $(6)(6) = 36$ man-days. Then, $36 \div 4 = 9$ days

9. Total cost = $(8)(3)(7)(\$16.245) + (3)(\$138.60) = \$3144.96$

10. Total cost = $(4)(6)(\$15.15)(8) + (4)(\$128.00) = \$3420.80$

11. $5/16 + 4/8 + 21/32 = 1.59375 \approx 1\text{-}594$

12. $(\$10.82)(40) + (\$16.23)(2) = \$465.26$

13. A: 70 ft/sec = (70/22)(15) = 47.73 mph; B: 50 mph; C: .9 mi/min. =44 (.9)(60) = 54 mph; D: 4500 ft/min = 75 ft/sec = (75/22)(15) ~ 51.14 mph So, C is fastest.

14. $(24-16) \div 24 = 1/3 \approx 33\%$

15. Let x = miles. Then, $15/60 = x/40$. Solving, $x = 10$

16. $(3)(60/6) = 30$ mph

17. Distance = $30/60 \times 2 \times 5280 = 5280$ ft.

18. 15 mph = 1 mi. in 4 min. If this 1 mi. is reduced to 3 min., then rate = 60/3 = 20 mph

19. $(8.3)(12) = 99.6 \approx 100$ miles. Note: 1 roundtrip = 16.6 miles

20. $(5)(2)(1\ 1/2) = 15$ min.

21. Let x, 2x = number of cars for the 3rd and 2nd tracks, respectively. Then, $x + 2x = 30$, so $x = 10$. Since the 1st track holds 30 cars, the 1st and 3rd tracks hold 40 cars.

22. 2 movements are required. Move the 3 cars on each track containing 3 cars over to the track (other one) containing 6 cars. However, from one of the tracks containing 3 cars, just move 1 car to the 6-car track (6+3+1 =10)

23. $[(24)(2)+(21)(2)] \div 6 = 15$ trains in a 10-minute period. We assume there are 2 local tracks and 2 express tracks.

24. Let x = mph. Then, 2/5 = x/60. Solving, x = 24

25. ($13.40)(8.5) = $113.90

TEST 2

DIRECTIONS: Each question or incomplete statement is followed by several suggested answers or completions. Select the one that BEST answers the question or completes the statement. *PRINT THE LETTER OF THE CORRECT ANSWER IN THE SPACE AT THE RIGHT.*

1. A trainmaster standing on a local station times the passing of an express train as 16 seconds.
   If the express was 610 feet long, its AVERAGE speed passing the trainmaster was _____ mph.

   A. 24   B. 26   C. 28   D. 30

   1._____

2. A trainmaster stations himself opposite the head end of a 440-foot-long local train which has stopped in the station. This train takes 28 seconds to pass the trainmaster after it has started.
   Considering that this is an actual rather than a theoretical train, the rear of the train passes the trainmaster at a speed which is CLOSEST to _____ mph.

   A. 10   B. 14   C. 18   D. 22

   2._____

3. A 12 1/2 percent increase on a $1.40 fare would be MOST closely approximated by charging fares at

   A. 5 for $7.87   B. 6 for $7.84
   C. 8 for $8.60   D. 10 for $16.80

   3._____

4. A special fare operation will require that 3 motormen, 4 conductors, and 2 towermen be assigned to this service on an 8-hour basis each day that the operation is in effect. Assuming that all other operating costs come to 25% of the wages of the personnel already specified, the MINIMUM number of daily passengers to just cover costs at a 40-cent fare would have to be

   A. 420   B. 540   C. 680   D. 800

   4._____

5. If a speed of 15 miles per hour is exactly 22 feet per second, then the number of miles per hour corresponding to 40 feet per second is MOST NEARLY

   A. 10   B. 20   C. 25   D. 30

   5._____

6. If the average speed of a train is 20 mph, the time it takes the train to travel 1 mile is _____ minutes.

   A. 2   B. 3   C. 4   D. 5

   6._____

7. If the average speed of a train between two stations is 30 miles per hour, and the two stations are 1/2 mile apart, the time it takes the train to travel from one station to the other is _____ minute(s).

   A. 1   B. 2   C. 3   D. 4

   7._____

8. A lay-up yard has five equal length tracks that can hold a total of 55 cars.
   If 8 cars are laid up on one track and six cars on each of the other four, the additional number of cars that can be laid up in this yard is

   A. 8   B. 23   C. 24   D. 32

   8._____

9. If twelve 10-car trains and eight 8-car trains pass a point on a certain track during one hour, the headway on that track is _____ minutes.

   A. 6 B. 5 C. 4 D. 3

10. The running time of a train between two terminals is 48 minutes, and there is a 7-minute layover at each terminal. If a train leaves one terminal at 11:00 A.M., this train is due back at the same terminal at

    A. 11:48 A.M. B. 11:55 A.M.
    C. 12:43 P.M. D. 12:50 P.M.

11. A motorman's weekly pay for 8 hours a day, 5 days a week, at $13.32 an hour is

    A. $533.20 B. $532.80 C. $528.80 D. $493.20

12. If seven 10-car trains and eight 8-car trains pass a point on a certain track during one hour, the headway on that track is _____ minutes. (Refer to note on page 2/Test 1.)

    A. 2 B. 4 C. 5 D. 6

13. If the average speed of a train is 30 miles per hour, the time it takes the train to travel one mile is _____ minutes.

    A. 2 B. 3 C. 4 D. 5

14. A 5-track lay-up yard can hold a total of 5 ten-car trains. There are already 5 cars stored on each of 4 tracks and 10 cars stored on the fifth track.
    The number of additional cars that can be stored in this yard is

    A. 20 B. 25 C. 30 D. 32

15. If a train takes 4 minutes to travel between 2 stations that are 1 mile apart, the average speed of the train is APPROXIMATELY _____ mph.

    A. 5 B. 15 C. 25 D. 35

16. A seven-track lay-up yard can hold 16 cars on each track, but there are already five 8-car trains in this yard.
    The number of additional cars that can be stored in this yard is

    A. 40 B. 60 C. 72 D. 112

17. A motorman's weekly pay for 8 hours a day, 5 days a week, at $13.50 an hour is

    A. $108.00 B. $480.00 C. $540.00 D. $555.00

18. A train moving at the rate of 24 miles per hour will travel 4 miles in _____ minutes.

    A. 6 B. 10 C. 20 D. 96

19. If a certain motorman earns $472.00 each week and works 40 hours each week, his rate of pay per hour is

    A. $11.50 B. $11.60 C. $11.70 D. $11.80

20. A train moving at the rate of 30 miles per hour will travel 6 miles in _____ minutes.

    A. 5 B. 8 C. 10 D. 12

21. A certain motorman reports for work at 8 A.M. on Tuesday and normally clears at 3:30 P.M. He is paid at the hourly rate of $11.80.
    What should his gross pay be for this day if, due to a train delay, he gets only 10 minutes for lunch?

    A. $94.40   B. $100.30   C. $104.20   D. $106.20

21.____

22. A certain towerman reports for work at 8 A.M. on Tuesday and normally clears at 3:30 P.M. He is paid at the hourly rate of $12.40. If it takes an hour to write a report, what is his gross pay for this day if he is required to write an unusual occurrence report at the end of his run?

    A. $99.20   B. $105.40   C. $110.40   D. $117.40

22.____

23. A motorman reports for work at 7 A.M. on Tuesday and normally clears at 2:30 P.M. He is paid at the hourly rate of $12.80.
    What is his gross pay for this day if he has a student motorman with him for an extra 2 1/2 hours?

    A. $102.40   B. $115.20   C. $128.00   D. $140.00

23.____

24. A certain conductor reports at 8 A.M. and normally clears at 3 P.M. His hourly rate of pay is $11.00.
    What should his gross pay be for this day if he is late at the end of his run and clears at 4 P.M.?

    A. $88.00   B. $92.50   C. $99.00   D. $102.50

24.____

25. The speed of a train that travels 6 miles in 12 minutes is_____ mph.

    A. 20   B. 30   C. 40   D. 50

25.____

KEY (CORRECT ANSWERS)

1.	B	11.	B
2.	D	12.	A
3.	A	13.	A
4.	C	14.	A
5.	C	15.	B
6.	B	16.	C
7.	A	17.	C
8.	B	18.	B
9.	D	19.	D
10.	C	20.	D

21. B
22. B
23. C
24. A
25. B

SOLUTIONS TO PROBLEMS

1. 610' in 16 sec. = (610')(225) = 137,250' in 1 hour. Then, 137,250 ÷ 5280 ≈ 26 mph

2. 440' in 28 sec. ≈ (440')(128.57) ≈ 56,571' in 1 hour. Then, 56,571 ÷ 5280 ≈ 11 mph average speed. Thus, the final speed can be found by solving for x: (0+x)/2 = 11. Solving, x = 22

3. ($1.40)(1.125) = $1.575. This is closest to 5 for $7.84, which is $1.568 apiece.

4. Can't be done. Insufficient information

5. (15)(40/22) = 27.27 mph, closest to 25 mph

6. 60/20 = 3min.

7. 30 nph means 1 min. to travel 1/2 mile

8. 55 - 8 - (6)(4) = 23 additional cars

9. (12)(10) + (8)(8) = 184. Then, 184 ÷ 60 ≈ 3 min.

10. 11:00 AM + 48 min. + 7 min. + 48 min. = 12:43 PM

11. (8)(5)($13.32) = $532.80

12. (7)(10) + (8)(8) = 134. Then, 134 ÷ 60 ≈ 2 min.

13. Let x = number of minutes. Then, 30/60 = 1/x . Solving, x = 2

14. 50 - (5)(4) - 10 = 20 additional cars

15. Let x = average speed in mph. Then, x/60 = 1/4. Solving, x = 15

16. (16)(7) - (5)(8) = 72 additional cars

17. (8)(5)($13.50) = $540.00

18. Let x = number of minutes. Then, 24/60=4/x . Solving, x = 10

19. $472.00 ÷ 40 = $11.80 per hour

20. Let x = number of minutes. Then, 30/60 = 6/x . Solving, x = 12

21. ($11.80)(8.5) = $100.30

22. ($12.40)(8.5) = $105.40

23. ($12.80X10) = $128.00

24. ($11.00)(8) = $88.00

25. Let x = speed in mph. Then, 6/12=x/60. Solving, x = 30

TEST 3

DIRECTIONS: Each question or incomplete statement is followed by several suggested answers or completions. Select the one that BEST answers the question or completes the statement. *PRINT THE LETTER OF THE CORRECT ANSWER IN THE SPACE AT THE RIGHT.*

1. A certain subway train on straight level track has an acceleration rate of 1.7 miles per hour per second up to 18 mph.
   The distance this train must travel on straight level track to accelerate from 8 mph to 18 mph is about _____ feet.

   A. 75   B. 95   C. 110   D. 140

2. The average service braking rate of the R-10 and later subway cars is 2.5 miles per hour per second whereas on earlier cars the service braking rate average 1.5 miles per hour per second.
   The number of seconds saved by the use of the newer equipment in service braking from 26 miles per hour to a stop is approximately

   A. 17.3   B. 10.4   C. 6.9   D. 3.5

3. Ninety percent of the 240 conductors and motormen reporting daily at a certain terminal are married, and 40% of all conductors and motormen are under 35 years of age.
   The MINIMUM number of married conductors and motormen in this lower age group is

   A. 48   B. 60   C. 72   D. 84

4. If a train having a length of 600 feet passes a point in 10 seconds, its speed, in miles per hour, is CLOSEST to

   A. 39   B. 41   C. 86   D. 88

5. A train is 450 feet long and travels at a rate of 45 mph. The length of time it takes this train to pass a certain point is CLOSEST to _____ seconds.

   A. 6.8   B. 7.0   C. 14.5   D. 14.7

6. The running time from terminal to terminal for a certain line is 50 minutes, and the relay time is 6 minutes at each terminal.
   How many additional cars are required to increase the present eight-car service to ten cars while maintaining the present headway of 8 minutes?

   A. 24   B. 26   C. 28   D. 30

7. The length of a train which passes a certain point in 15 seconds while moving at a speed of 20 mph is _____ feet.

   A. 204   B. 210   C. 440   D. 450

8. The average speed of a train between two terminals 6 miles apart is 12 mph.
   The time required to make one roundtrip allowing 15 minutes for relay time at the far terminal is _____ minutes.

   A. 60   B. 65   C. 70   D. 75

9. Each track of a four track lay-up yard can hold 10 cars. There are a total of 10 cars already in this yard.
   The number of additional cars that can be stored in this yard is

   A. 35   B. 30   C. 25   D. 20

10. What is the speed of a train that travels five miles in ten minutes? _____ mph.

    A. 24   B. 25   C. 28   D. 30

11. If a certain conductor earns $360.00 a week and works 40 hours, his salary per hour is

    A. $10.00   B. $8.50   C. $9.00   D. $9.50

12. A conductor earns $10.82 per hour. He is paid time and one-half for each hour worked over 40 hours per week. If a conductor works 44 hours in one week, his gross salary for that week is

    A. $497.68   B. $497.72   C. $499.72   D. $499.92

13. An 8-car subway train consisting of 75-foot cars took 60 seconds to enter and clear a 620-foot station without stopping.
    The speed of this train was MOST NEARLY _____ mph.

    A. 7   B. 14   C. 18   D. 28

14. A certain motorman reports at 8:00 A.M. and normally clears at 3:30 P.M. His hourly rate of pay is $12.40. What should his gross pay be for this day if he is late at the end of his run and clears at 4:30 P.M.?

    A. $105.40   B. $111.60   C. $114.00   D. $117.80

15. The FASTEST of the following speeds is

    A. 85 feet per second
    B. 0.95 mile per minute
    C. 57 miles per hour
    D. 5,000 feet per minute

16. An eight-car train leaves a terminal carrying in each car, respectively, passenger loads of 173, 182, 147, 152, 145, 148, 180, and 170.
    Using a capacity of 210 passengers per car, the AVERAGE passenger loading per car is about

    A. 70%   B. 77%   C. 80%   D. 85%

17. For certain cars, the service braking distance is about 40% greater when fully loaded than when empty.
    If the fully loaded service braking distance from 35 mph is 465 feet, the service braking distance for empty cars under the same conditions should be about _____ feet.

    A. 185   B. 280   C. 330   D. 650

18. A special fare operation requires that 4 motormen, 6 conductors, and 2 towermen be assigned to the service. The men start at 8:00 A.M. and clear at 3:45 P.M. The rate of pay for a motorman is $18 per hour, for a conductor $16 per hour, and for a towerman $17.60 per hour. The 12 men have no other assignments.
Assuming that all other operating costs come to 25% of the wages of the personnel already specified, the MINIMUM number of daily passengers to just cover cost at $3.00 fare would have to be NEAREST to

    A. 600   B. 660   C. 720   D. 770

19. The roundtrip time between two terminals, not including layover time, is 1 hour, 20 minutes.
A train due to arrive at one terminal at 9:10 should leave the other terminal at

    A. 7:50   B. 8:00   C. 8:10   D. 8:30

20. An express train requires five minutes to make the run between two stations which are two and one-half miles apart.
The AVERAGE speed of the train for this run is _____ mph.

    A. 24   B. 30   C. 36   D. 42

21. If twenty 10-car trains and ten 8-car trains pass a point on a certain track during one hour, the headway on that track, in minutes, is (See note in Test 1, question 12.)

    A. 1 1/2   B. 2   C. 3   D. 5

22. If the average speed of a train is 30 miles per hour, the time it takes the train to travel one mile is _____ minute(s).

    A. 1   B. 2   C. 3   D. 4

23. A 5-track lay-up yard can hold a total of 5 ten-car trains. There are already 3 cars stored on each of 4 tracks and 4 cars stored on the fifth track.
The number of additional cars that can be stored in this yard is

    A. 14   B. 24   C. 34   D. 44

24. A six-track lay-up yard can hold 12 cars on each track but there are already four 10-car trains in this yard.
The number of additional cars that can be stored in this yard is

    A. 12   B. 32   C. 40   D. 72

25. An express train requires five minutes to make the run between two stations which are two miles apart.
The AVERAGE speed of the train, in miles per hour, for this run is

    A. 20   B. 24   C. 30   D. 36

KEY (CORRECT ANSWERS)

1.	C	11.	C
2.	C	12.	B
3.	C	13.	B
4.	B	14.	A
5.	A	15.	A
6.	C	16.	B
7.	C	17.	C
8.	D	18.	B
9.	B	19.	D
10.	D	20.	B

21. D
22. B
23. C
24. B
25. B

SOLUTIONS TO PROBLEMS

1. 8 mph = 11.7$\overline{3}$ ft/sec, 1.7 m/hr/sec = 2.49$\overline{3}$ ft/sec^2. The formula for distance is d = vt + 1/2gt^2, where v = the initial velocity, g = rate of acceleration, and t = time. To determine time, t = (18-8.) ÷ 1.7 ≈ 5.88 sec. Thus, d = (11.73)(5.88) + (1/2)(2.49$\overline{3}$)(5.88^2) ≈ 112 ft., closest to 110 ft,

2. For the R-10, the time = (26-0) ÷ 2.5 = 10.4 *sec.*, whereas the time for the earlier cars = (26-0) ÷ 1.5 = 17.$\overline{3}$ sec. The time saved is approximately 6.9 sec. (Actual time = 6.9$\overline{3}$ sec)

3. Let x = number of individuals both married and under 35 years old. Then, the number of individuals married but NOT under 35 years old = (.90)(240) - x = 216 - x. Likewise, the number of individuals under 35 years old but not married = (.40)(240) - x = 96 - x. Thus, (216-x) + x + (96-x) ≤ 240. Solving, x ≥ 72

4. Let x = speed in mph. Then, 600/10 = y/3600. Thus, y = 216,000 ft/hr. To find x, divide y by 5280. So, x ≈ 41

5. 45 mph = 66 ft/sec. Then, 450 ÷ 66 ≈ 6.8 sec.

6. Unable to solve

7. 20 mph = 29 1/3 ft/sec. Then, (29 1/3)(15) = 440 ft.

8. At 12 mph, 6 miles can be traveled in 1/2 hour (or 30 minutes). Then, 30 + 15 + 30 = 75 minutes.

9. (10)(4) - 10 = 30 additional cars

10. 5 miles in 10 minutes = (5)(6) = 30 mph

11. $360.00 ÷ 40 = $9.00 per hour

12. ($10.82)(40) + ($16.23)(4) = $497.72

13. (8)(75) = 600 ft. The train went 600 + 620 = 1220 ft. in 1 minute. This is equivalent to 73,200 ft. per hour. Finally, 73,200 ÷ 5280 ≈ 14 mph.

14. (8.5)($12.40) = $105.40

15. A: 85 ft/sec = (85/88)(60) ≈ 57.95 mph; B: .95 mi/min = (.95)(60) = 57 mph; C: As is 57 mph; D: 5000 ft/min = 83.$\overline{3}$ ft/sec = (83$\overline{3}$/88)(60) ≈ 56-82 mph. Thus, A is fastest.

16. (173+182+147+152+145+148+180+170) ÷ 8 = 162.125 Then, 162.125 ÷ 210 ≈ 77%

17. 465 ÷ 1.40 ≈ 332 ft., closest to 330 ft.

18. (4)(7.75)($18) + (6)(7.75)($16) + (2)(7.75)($17.60) = $1574.80.
    Now, (1.25)(1574.80) = 1,968.50.
    Finally, $1,968.50 ÷ $3.00 = 656.16, closest to 660 passengers.

19. (1 hr. 20 min.) ÷ 2 = 40 minutes. Then, 9:10 - 40 min. = 8:30

20. 2 1/2 miles in 5 minutes = (2 1/2)(12) = 30 mph

21. [(20)(10)+(10)(8)] ÷ 60 = 4 2/3 ≈ 5 min.

22. 30 mph = 60/30 = 2 min, to travel 1 mile

23. (5)(10) - (3)(4) - (4)(1) = 34 additional cars

24. (6)(12) - (4)(10) = 32 additional cars

25. 2 miles in 5 minutes means (2)(60/5) = 24 mph

SUPERVISION, ADMINISTRATION, MANAGEMENT AND ORGANIZATION
EXAMINATION SECTION

TEST 1

DIRECTIONS: Each question or incomplete statement is followed by several suggested answers or completions. Select the one that BEST answers the question or completes the statement. *PRINT THE LETTER OF THE CORRECT ANSWER IN THE SPACE AT THE RIGHT.*

1. The one of the following practices by a supervisor which is MOST likely to lead to confusion and inefficiency is for him to
   A. give orders verbally directly to the man assigned to the job
   B. issue orders only in writing
   C. follow up his orders after issuing them
   D. relay his orders to the men through co-workers

2. If you are given an oral order by a supervisor which you do not understand completely, you should
   A. use your own judgment
   B. discuss the order with your men
   C. ask your supervisor for a further explanation
   D. carry out that part of the order which you do understand and then ask for more information

3. An orientation program for a group of new employees should NOT ordinarily include a
   A. review of the organizational structure of the agency
   B. detailed description of the duties of each new employee
   C. description of the physical layout of the repair shop
   D. statement of the rules pertaining to sick leave, vacation, and holidays

4. The MOST important rule to follow with regard to discipline is that a man should be disciplined
   A. after everyone has had time to "cool off"
   B. as soon as possible after the infraction of rules
   C. only for serious rule violations
   D. before he makes a mistake

5. If the men under your supervision continue to work effectively even when you are out sick for several days, it would MOST probably indicate that
   A. the men are merely trying to show you up
   B. the men are in constant fear of you and are glad you are away
   C. you have trained your men properly and have their full cooperation
   D. you are serving no useful purpose since the men can get along without you

6. When evaluating subordinates, the employee who should be rated HIGHEST by his supervisor is the one who
   A. never lets the supervisor do heavy lifting
   B. asks many questions about the work
   C. makes many suggestions on work procedures
   D. listens to instructions and carries them out

7. Of the following, the factor which is generally MOST important to the conduct of successful training is
   A. time   B. preparation   C. equipment   D. space

8. One of the MAJOR disadvantages of "on-the-job" training is that it
   A. requires a long training period for instructors
   B. may not be progressive
   C. requires additional equipment
   D. may result in the waste of supplies

9. For a supervisor to train workers in several trades which involve various skills, presents many training problems.
   The one of the following which is NOT true in such a training situation is that
   A. less supervision is required
   B. greater planning for training is required
   C. rotation of assignments is necessary
   D. less productivity can be expected

10. For a supervisor of repair workers to have each worker specialize in learning a single trade is GENERALLY
    A. *desirable*; each worker will become expert in his assigned trade
    B. *undesirable*; there is less flexibility of assignments possible when each worker has learned only a single trade
    C. *desirable*; the training responsibility of the supervisor is simplified when each worker is required to learn a single trade
    D. *undesirable*; workers lose interest quickly when they know they are expected to learn a single trade

11. An IMPORTANT advantage of standardizing work procedures is that it
    A. develops all-around skills
    B. makes the work less monotonous
    C. provides an incentive for good work
    D. enable the work to be done with less supervision

12. Generally, the GREATEST difficulty in introducing new work methods is due to the fact that
    A. men become set in their ways
    B. the old way is generally better
    C. only the department will benefit from changes
    D. explaining new methods is time consuming

13. Assume that you are required to transmit an order with, which you do not agree, to your subordinates.
    In this case, it would be BEST for you to
    A. ask one of your superiors to transmit the order
    B. refuse to transmit an order with which you do not agree
    C. transmit the order but be sure to explain that you do not agree with it
    D. transmit the order and enforce it to the best of your ability

13.____

14. The MAIN reason for written orders is that
    A. proper blame can be placed if the order is not carried out
    B. the order will be carried out faster
    C. the order can be properly analyzed as to its meaning
    D. there will be no doubt as to what the order says

14.____

15. You have been informed unofficially by another shop manager that some of the men under your supervision are loafing on the job.
    This situation can be BEST handled by
    A. telling the man to mind his own business
    B. calling the men together and reprimanding them
    C. having the men work under your direct supervision
    D. arranging to make spot checks at more frequent intervals

15.____

16. Suggestions on improving methods of doing work, when submitted by a new employee, should be
    A. examined for possible merit because the new man may have a fresh viewpoint
    B. ignored because it would make the old employees resentful
    C. disregarded because he is too unfamiliar with the work
    D. examined only for the purpose of judging the new man

16.____

17. One of your employees often slows down the work of his crew by playing practical jokes.
    The BEST way to handle this situation is to
    A. arrange for his assignment to more than his share of unpleasant jobs
    B. warn him that he must stop this practice at once
    C. ignore this situation for he will soon tire of it
    D. ask your supervisor to transfer him

17.____

18. One of your men is always complaining about working conditions, equipment, and his fellow workers.
    The BEST action for you to take in this situation is to
    A. have this man work alone if possible
    B. consider each complaint on is merits
    C. tell him bluntly that you will not listen to any of his complaints
    D. give this man the worst jobs until he quits complaining

18.____

19. It is generally agreed that men who are interested in their work will do the best work.
    A supervisor can LEAST stimulate this interest by
    A. complimenting men on good work
    B. correcting men on their working procedures
    C. striving to create overtime for his men
    D. recommending merit raises for excellent work

20. If you, as a supervisor, have criticized one of your men for making a mistake, you should
    A. remind the man of his error from time to time to keep him on his toes
    B. overlook any further errors which this man may make, otherwise he may feel he is a victim of discrimination
    C. give the man the opportunity to redeem himself
    D. impress the man with the fact that all his work will be closely checked from then on

21. In his efforts to maintain standards of performance, a shop manager uses a system of close supervision to detect or catch errors.
    An *opposite* method of accomplishing the *same* objective is to employ a program which
    A. instills in each employee a pride of workmanship to do the job correctly the first time
    B. groups each job accordingly to the importance to the overall objectives of the program
    C. makes the control of quality the responsibility of an inspector
    D. emphasizes that there is a "one" best way for an employee to do s specific job

22. Assume that after taking over a repair shop, a shop manager feels that he is taking too much time maintaining records.
    He should
    A. temporarily assign this job to one of his senior repair crew chiefs
    B. get together with his supervisor to determine if all these records are needed
    C. stop keeping those records which he believes are unnecessary
    D. spend a few additional hours each day until his records are current

23. In order to apply performance standards to employees engaged in repair shop activities, a shop manager must FIRST
    A. allow workers to decide for themselves the way to do the job
    B. determine what is acceptable as satisfactory work
    C. separate the more difficult tasks from the simpler tasks
    D. stick to an established work schedule

5 (#1)

24. Of the following actions a shop manager can take to determine whether the vehicles used in his shop are being utilized properly, the one which will give him the LEAST meaningful information is
    A. conducting an analysis of vehicle assignments
    B. reviewing the number of miles traveled by each vehicle with and without loads
    C. recording the unloaded weights of each vehicle
    D. comparing the amount of time vehicles are parked at job sites with the time required to travel to and from job sites

24.____

25. For a shop manager, the MOST important reason that equipment which is used infrequently should be considered for disposal is that
    A. the time required for its maintenance could be better used elsewhere
    B. such equipment may cause higher management to think that your shop is not busy
    C. the men may resent having to work on such equipment
    D. such equipment usually has a higher breakdown rate in operation

25.____

KEY (CORRECT ANSWERS)

1.	D	11.	D
2.	C	12.	A
3.	B	13.	D
4.	B	14.	D
5.	C	15.	D
6.	D	16.	A
7.	B	17.	B
8.	B	18.	B
9.	A	19.	C
10.	B	20.	C

21. A
22. B
23. B
24. C
25. A

TEST 2

DIRECTIONS: Each question or incomplete statement is followed by several suggested answers or completions. Select the one that BEST answers the question or completes the statement. *PRINT THE LETTER OF THE CORRECT ANSWER IN THE SPACE AT THE RIGHT.*

1. Assume that one of your subordinates approaches you with a grievance concerning working conditions.
   Of the following, the BEST action for you to take first is to
   A. "soft-soap" him, since most grievances are imaginary
   B. settle the grievance to his satisfaction
   C. try to talk him out of his complaint
   D. listen patiently and sincerely to the complaint

   1.____

2. Of the following, the BEST way for a supervisor to help a subordinate learn a new skill which requires the use of tools is for him to give this subordinate
   A. a list of good books on the subject
   B. lectures on the theoretical aspects of the task
   C. opportunities to watch someone using the tools
   D. opportunities to practice the skill, under close supervision

   2.____

3. A supervisor finds that his own work load is excessive because several of his subordinates are unable to complete their assignments.
   Of the following, the BEST action for him to take to improve this situation is to
   A. discipline these subordinates
   B. work overtime
   C. request additional staff
   D. train these subordinates in more efficient work methods

   3.____

4. The one of the following situations which is MOST likely to be the result of *poor* morale is a(n)
   A. high rate of turnover
   B. decrease in number of requests by subordinates for transfers
   C. increase in the backlog of work
   D. decrease in the rate of absenteeism

   4.____

5. As a supervisor, you find that several of your subordinates are not meeting their deadlines because they are doing work assigned to them by one of your fellow supervisors without your knowledge.
   Of the following, the BEST course of action for you to take in this situation is to
   A. tell the other supervisors to make future assignments through you
   B. assert your authority by publicly telling the other supervisors to stop issuing orders to your workers
   C. go along with this practice; it is an effective way to fully utilize the available manpower
   D. take the matter directly to your immediate supervisor without delay

   5.____

2 (#2)

6. If a supervisor of a duplicating section in an agency hears a rumor concerning a change in agency personnel policy through the "grapevine," he should
    A. *repeat* it to his subordinates so they will be informed
    B. *not repeat* it to his subordinates before he determines the facts because, as supervisor, his work may give it unwarranted authority
    C. *repeat* it to his subordinates so that they will like him for confiding in them
    D. *not repeat* it to his subordinates before he determines the facts because a duplicating section is not concerned with matters of policy

6.____

7. When teaching a new employee how to operate a machine, a supervisor should FIRST
    A. let the employee try to operate the machine by himself, since he can learn only by his mistakes
    B. explain the process to him with the use of diagrams before showing him the machine
    C. have him memorize the details of the operation from the manual
    D. explain and demonstrate the various steps in the process, making sure he understands each step

7.____

8. If a subordinate accuses you of always giving him the least desirable assignments, you should IMMEDIATELY
    A. tell him that it is not true and you do not want to hear any more about it
    B. try to get specific details from him, so that you can find out what his impressions are based on
    C. tell him that you distribute assignments in the fairest way possible and he must be mistaken
    D. ask him what current assignment he has that he does not like, and assign it to someone else

8.____

9. Suppose that the production of an operator under your supervision has been unsatisfactory and you have decided to have a talk with him about it.
During the interview, it would be BEST for you to
    A. discuss only the subordinate's weak points so that he can overcome them
    B. discuss only the subordinate's strong points so that he will not become discouraged
    C. compare the subordinate's work with that of his co-workers so that he will know what is expected of him
    D. discuss both his weak and strong points so that he will get a view of his overall performance

9.____

10. Suppose that an operator under your supervision makes a mistake in color on a 2,000-page job and runs it on white paper instead of on blue paper.
Of the following, your BEST course in these circumstances would be to point out the error to the operator and
    A. have the operator rerun the job immediately on blue paper
    B. send the job to the person who ordered it without comment
    C. send the job to the person who ordered it and tell him it could not be done on blue paper
    D. ask the person who ordered the job whether the white paper is acceptable

10.____

11. Assuming that all your subordinates have equal technical competence, the BEST policy for a supervisor to follow when making assignments of undesirable jobs would be to
    A. distribute them as evenly as possible among his subordinates
    B. give them to the subordinate with the poorest attendance record
    C. ask the subordinate with the least seniority to do them
    D. assign them to the subordinate who is least likely to complain

12. To get the BEST results when training a number of subordinates at the same time, a supervisor should
    A. treat all of them in an identical manner to avoid accusations of favoritism
    B. treat them all fairly, but use different approaches in dealing with people of different personality types
    C. train only one subordinate, and have him train the others, because this will save a lot of the supervisor's time
    D. train first the subordinates who learn quickly so as to make the others think that the operation is easy to learn

13. Assume that, after a week's vacation, you return to find that one of your subordinates has produced a job which is unsatisfactory.
    Your BEST course of action at that time would be to
    A. talk to your personnel department about implementing disciplinary action
    B. discuss unsatisfactory work in the unit at a meeting with all of your subordinates
    C. discuss the job with the subordinate to determine why he was unable to do it properly
    D. ignore the matter, because it is too late to correct the mistake

14. Suppose that an operator under your supervision informs you that Mr. Y, a senior administrator in your agency, has been submitting for copying many papers which are obviously personal in nature. The operator wants to know what to do about it, since the duplication of personal papers is against agency rules.
    Your BEST course of action in these circumstances would be to
    A. tell the operator to pretend not to notice the content of the material and continue to copy whatever is given to him
    B. tell the operator that Mr. Y, as a senior administrator, must have gotten special permission to have personal papers duplicated
    C. have the operator refer Mr. Y to you and inform Mr. Y yourself that duplication of personal papers is against agency rules
    D. call Mr. Y's superior and tell him that Mr. Y has been having personal papers duplicated, which is against agency rules

15. Assume that you are teaching a certain process to an operator under your supervision.
    In order to BEST determine whether he is actually learning what you are teaching, you should ask questions which
    A. can easily be answered by a "yes" or "no"
    B. require or encourage guessing

C. require a short description of what has been taught
D. are somewhat ambiguous so as to make the learner think about the procedures in question

16. If an employee is chronically late or absent, as his supervisor, it would be BEST for you to
    A. let his work pile up so he can see that no one else will do it for him
    B. discuss the matter with him and stress the importance of finding a solution
    C. threaten to enter a written report on the matter into his personnel file
    D. work out a system with him so he can have a different work schedule than the other employees

17. Assume that you have a subordinate who has just finished a basic training course in the operation of a machine.
    Giving him a large and difficult FIRST assignment would be
    A. *good*, because it would force him to "learn the ropes"
    B. *bad*, because he would probably have difficulty in carrying it out, discouraging him and resulting in a waste of time and supplies
    C. *good*, because how he handles it would give you an excellent basis for judging his competence
    D. *bad*, because he would probably assume that you are discriminating against him

18. After putting a new employee under your supervision through an initial training period, assigning him to work with a more experienced employee for a while would be a
    A. *good* idea, because it would give him the opportunity to observe what he had been taught and to participate in production himself
    B. *bad* idea, because he should not be required to work under the direction of anyone who is not his supervisor
    C. *good* idea, because it would raise the morale of the more experienced employee who could use him to do all the unpleasant chores
    D. *bad* idea, because the best way for him to learn would be to give him full responsibility for assignments right away

19. Assume that a supervisor is responsible for ordering supplies for the duplicating section in his agency.
    Which one of the following actions would be MOST helpful in determining when to place orders so that an adequate supply of materials will be on hand at all times?
    A. Taking an inventory of supplies on hand at least every two months
    B. Asking his subordinates to inform him when they see that supplies are low
    C. Checking the inventory of supplies whenever he has time
    D. Keeping a running inventory of supplies and a record of estimated needs

5 (#2)

20. Routine procedures that have worked well in the past should be reviewed periodically by a supervisor MAINLY because
    A. they may have become outdated or in need of revision
    B. employees might dislike the procedures even though they have proven successful in the past
    C. these reviews are the main part of a supervisor's job
    D. this practice serves to give the supervisor an idea of how productive his subordinates are

20.____

21. Assume that an employee tells his supervisor about a grievance he has against a co-worker. The supervisor assures the employee that he will immediately take action to eliminate the grievance.
    The supervisor's attitude should be considered
    A. *correct*, because a good supervisor is one who can come to a quick decision
    B. *incorrect*, because the supervisor should have told the employee that he will investigate the grievance and then determine a future course of action
    C. *correct*, because the employee's morale will be higher, resulting in greater productivity
    D. *incorrect*, because the supervisor should remain uninvolved and let the employees settle grievances between themselves

21.____

22. If an employee's work output is low and of poor quality due to faulty work habits, the MOST constructive of the following ways for a supervisor to correct this situation generally is to
    A. discipline the employee
    B. transfer the employee to another unit
    C. provide additional training
    D. check the employee's work continuously

22.____

23. Assume that it becomes necessary for a supervisor to ask his staff to work overtime.
    Which one of the following techniques is MOST likely to win their willing cooperation to do this?
    A. Explain that this is part of their job specification entitled, "performs related work"
    B. Explain the reason it is necessary for the employees to work overtime
    C. Promise the employees special consideration regarding future leave matters
    D. Explain that if the employees do not work overtime, they will face possible disciplinary action

23.____

24. If an employee's work performance has recently fallen below established minimum standards for quality and quantity, the threat of demotion or other disciplinary measures as an attempt to improve this employee's performance would probably be the MOST acceptable and effective course of action
    A. *only* after other more constructive measures have failed
    B. *if* applied uniformly to all employees as soon as performance falls below standard

24.____

25. If, as a supervisor, it becomes necessary for you to assign an employee to supervise your unit during your vacation, it would generally be BEST to select the employee who
    A. is the best technician on the staff
    B. can get the work out smoothly, without friction
    C. has the most seniority
    D. is the most popular with the group

KEY (CORRECT ANSWERS)

1.	D		11.	A
2.	D		12.	B
3.	D		13.	C
4.	A		14.	C
5.	A		15.	C
6.	B		16.	B
7.	D		17.	B
8.	B		18.	A
9.	D		19.	D
10.	D		20.	A

21. B
22. C
23. B
24. A
25. B

TEST 3

DIRECTIONS: Each question or incomplete statement is followed by several suggested answers or completions. Select the one that BEST answers the question or completes the statement. *PRINT THE LETTER OF THE CORRECT ANSWER IN THE SPACE AT THE RIGHT.*

1. An employee under your supervision has demonstrated a deep-seated personality problem that has begun to affect his work.
   This situation should be
      A. *ignored*, mainly because such problems usually resolve themselves
      B. *handled*, mainly because the employee should be assisted in seeking professional help
      C. *ignored*, mainly because the employee will consider any advice as interference
      D. *handled*, mainly because the supervisors should be qualified to resolve deep-seated personality problems

   1.____

2. Of the following, a supervisor will usually be MOST successful in maintaining employee morale while providing effective leadership if he
      A. takes prompt disciplinary action every time it is needed
      B. gives difficult assignments only to those workers who ask for such work
      C. promises his workers anything reasonable they request
      D. relies entirely on his staff for decisions

   2.____

3. When a supervisor makes an assignment to his subordinates, he should include a clear statement of what results are expected when the assignment is completed.
   Of the following, the BEST reason for following this procedure is that it will
      A. make it unnecessary for the supervisor to check on the progress of the work
      B. stimulate initiative and cooperation on the part of the more responsible workers
      C. give the subordinates a way to judge whether their work is meeting the requirements
      D. give the subordinates the feeling that they have some freedom of action

   3.____

4. Assume that, on a new employee's first day of work, his supervisor gives him a good orientation by telling him the general regulations and procedures used in the office and introducing him to his department head and fellow employees.
   For the remainder of the day, it would be BEST for the supervisor to
      A. give him steady instruction in all phases of his job, while stressing its most important aspects
      B. have him observe a fellow employee perform the duties of the job
      C. instruct him in that part of the job which he would prefer to learn first
      D. give him a simple task which requires little instruction and allows him to familiarize himself with the surroundings

   4.____

5. When it becomes necessary to criticize subordinates because several errors in the unit's work have been discovered, the supervisor should USUALLY
    A. focus on the job operation and avoid placing personal blame
    B. make every effort to fix blame and admonish the person responsible
    C. include in the criticism those employees who recognize and rectify their own mistakes
    D. repeat the criticism at regular intervals in order to impress the subordinates with the seriousness of their errors

6. If two employees under your supervision are continually bickering and cannot get along together, the FIRST action that you should take is to
    A. investigate possible ways of separating them
    B. ask your immediate superior for the procedure to follow in this situation
    C. determine the cause of their difficulty
    D. develop a plan and tell both parties to try it

7. In general, it is appropriate to recommend the transfer of an employee for all of the following reasons EXCEPT
    A. rewarding him
    B. providing him with a more challenging job
    C. remedying an error in initial placement
    D. disciplining him

8. Of the following, the MAIN disadvantage of basing a training and development program on a series of lectures is that the lecture technique
    A. does not sufficiently involve trainees in the learning process
    B. is more costly than other methods of training
    C. cannot be used to facilitate the understanding of difficult information
    D. is time consuming and inefficient

9. A supervisor has been assigned to train a new employee who is properly motivated but has made many mistakes.
    In the interview between the supervisor and employee about this problem, the employee should FIRST be
    A. asked if he can think of anything that he can do to improve his work
    B. complimented sincerely on some aspect of his work that is satisfactory
    C. asked to explain why he made the mistake
    D. advised that he may be dismissed if he continues to be careless

10. In training subordinates for more complex work, a supervisor must be aware of the progress that the subordinates are making.
    Determination of the results that have been accomplished by training is a concept commonly known as
    A. reinforcement
    B. feedback
    C. cognitive dissonance
    D. the halo effect

11. Assume that one of your subordinates loses interest in his work because he feels that your recent evaluation of his performance was unfair.
    The one of the following which is the BEST way to help him is to
    A. establish frequent deadlines for his work
    B. discuss his feelings and attitude with him
    C. discuss with him only the positive aspects of his performance
    D. arrange for his transfer to another unit

12. Informal organizations often develop at work.
    Of the following, the supervisor should realize that these groups will USUALLY
    A. determine work pace through unofficial agreements
    B. restrict vital communication channels
    C. lower morale by providing a chance to spread grievances
    D. provide leaders who will substitute for the supervisor when he is absent

13. Assume that you, the supervisor, have called to your office a subordinate whom, on several recent occasions, you have seen using the office telephone for personal use.
    In this situation, it would be MOST appropriate to begin the interview by
    A. discussing the disciplinary action that you believe to be warranted
    B. asking the subordinate to explain the reason for his personal use of the office telephone
    C. telling the subordinate about other employees who were disciplined for the same offense
    D. informing the subordinate that he is not to use the office telephone under any circumstances until further notice

14. Of the following, the success of any formal training program depends PRIMARILY upon the
    A. efficient and thorough preparation of materials, facilities, and procedures for instruction
    B. training program's practical relevance to the on-the-job situation
    C. scheduling of training sessions so as to minimize interference with normal job responsibilities
    D. creation of a positive initial reception on the part of the trainees

15. All of the following are legitimate purposes for regularly evaluating employee performance EXCEPT
    A. stimulating improvement in performance
    B. developing more accurate standards to be used in future ratings
    C. encouraging a spirit of competition
    D. allowing the employee to set realistic work goals for himself

16. A certain supervisor is very conscientious. He wants to receive personally all reports, correspondence, etc., and to be completely involved in all of the unit's operations. However, he is having difficulty in keeping up with the growing amount of paperwork.

Of the following, the MOST desirable course of action for him to take is to
A. put in more hours on the job
B. ask for additional office help
C. begin to delegate more of his work
D. inquire of his supervisor if the paperwork is really necessary

17. Assume that you are a supervisor. One of the workers under your supervision expresses his need to speak to you about a client who has been particularly uncooperative in providing information.
The MOST appropriate action for you to take FIRST would be to
A. agree to see the client for the worker in order to get the information
B. advise the worker to try several more times to get the information before he asks you for help
C. tell the worker you will go with him to see the client in order to observe his technique
D. ask the worker some questions in order to determine the type of help he needs in the situation

18. The supervisor who is MOST likely to achieve a high level of productivity from the professional employees under his supervision is the one who
A. watches their progress continuously
B. provides them with just enough information to carry out their assigned tasks
C. occasionally pitches in and helps them with their work
D. shares with them responsibility for setting work goals

19. Assume that there has been considerable friction for some time among the workers of a certain unit. The supervisor in charge of this unit becomes aware that the problem is getting serious as shown by increased absenteeism and lateness, loud arguments, etc.
Of the following, the BEST course of action for the supervisor to take FIRST is to
A. have a staff discussion about objectives and problems
B. seek out and penalize the apparent trouble-makers
C. set up and enforce stricter formal rules
D. discipline the next subordinate who causes friction

20. Assume that an employee under your supervision asks you for some blank paper and pencils to take home to her young grandson who, she says, delights in drawing.
The one of the following actions you SHOULD take is to
A. give her the material she wants and refrain from any comment
B. refuse her request and tell her that the use of office supplies for personal reasons is not proper
C. give her the material but suggest that she buy it next time
D. tell her to take the material herself since you do not want to know anything about the matter

21. A certain supervisor is given a performance evaluation by his superior. In it he is commended for his method of "delegation," a term that USUALLY refers to the action of
    A. determining the priorities for activities which must be completed
    B. assigning to subordinates some of the duties for which he is responsible
    C. standardizing operations in order to achieve results as close as possible to established goals
    D. dividing the activities necessary to achieve an objective into simple steps

22. A supervisor is approached by a subordinate who complains that a fellow worker is not assuming his share of the workload and is, therefore, causing more work for others in the office.
    Of the following, the MOST appropriate action for the supervisor to take in response to this complaint is to tell the subordinate
    A. that he will look into the matter
    B. to concentrate on his own job and not to worry about others
    C. to discuss the matter with the other worker
    D. that not everyone is capable of working at the same pace

23. Aside from the formal relationships established by management, informal and unofficial relationships will be developed among the personnel within an organization.
    Of the following, the MAIN importance of such informal relationships to the operations of the formal organization is that they
    A. reinforce the basic goals of the formal organization
    B. insure the interchangeability of the personnel within the organization
    C. provide an additional channel of communications within the organization
    D. insure predictability and control of the behavior of members of the organization

24. The most productive worker in a unit frequently takes overly-long coffee breaks and lunch hours while maintaining his above-average rate of productivity.
    Of the following, it would be MOST advisable for the supervisor to
    A. reprimand him, because rules must be enforced equally regardless of the merit of an individual's job performance
    B. ignore the infractions because a superior worker should be granted extra privileges for his efforts
    C. take no action unless others in the unit complain, because a reprimand may hurt the superior worker's feelings and cause him to produce less
    D. tell other members of the unit that a comparable rate of productivity on their part will be rewarded with similar privileges

25. A supervisor has been asked by his superior to choose an employee to supervise a special project.
Of the following, the MOST significant factor to consider in making this choice is the employee's

    A. length of service
    B. ability to do the job
    C. commitment to the goals of the agency
    D. attitude toward his fellow workers

25.____

KEY (CORRECT ANSWERS)

1.	B	11.	B
2.	A	12.	A
3.	C	13.	B
4.	D	14.	B
5.	A	15.	C
6.	C	16.	C
7.	D	17.	D
8.	A	18.	D
9.	B	19.	A
10.	B	20.	B

21.	B
22.	A
23.	C
24.	A
25.	B

TEST 4

DIRECTIONS: Each question or incomplete statement is followed by several suggested answers or completions. Select the one that BEST answers the question or completes the statement. *PRINT THE LETTER OF THE CORRECT ANSWER IN THE SPACE AT THE RIGHT.*

1. Assume that you are a newly appointed supervisor. 1.____
   Your MOST important responsibility is to
   A. make certain that all of the employees under your supervision are treated equally
   B. reduce disciplinary situations to a minimum
   C. insure an atmosphere of mutual trust between your workers and yourself
   D. see that the required work is done properly

2. In order to make sure that work is completed on time, the supervisor should 2.____
   A. pitch in and do as much of the work herself as she can
   B. schedule the work and control its progress
   C. not assign more than one person to any one task
   D. assign the same amount of work to each subordinate

3. Assume that you are a supervisor in charge of a number of workers who do the same kind of work and who each produce about the same volume of work in a given period of time. 3.____
   When their performance is evaluated, the worker who should be rated as the MOST accurate is the one
   A. whose errors are the easiest to correct
   B. whose errors involve the smallest amount of money
   C. who makes the fewest errors in her work
   D. who makes fewer errors as she becomes more experienced

4. As a supervisor, you have been asked by the manager to recommend whether the work of the bookkeeping office requires a permanent increase in bookkeeping office staff. 4.____
   Of the following questions, the one whose answer would be MOST likely to assist you in making your recommendation is:
   A. Are temporary employees hired to handle seasonal fluctuations in work loads?
   B. Are some permanent employees working irregular hours because they occasionally work overtime?
   C. Are the present permanent employees keeping the work of the bookkeeping office current?
   D. Are employees complaining that the work is unevenly divided?

5. Assume that you are a supervisor. One of your subordinates tells you that he is dissatisfied with his work assignment and that he wishes to discuss the matter with you. The employee is obviously very angry and upset.
   Of the following, the course of action that you should take FIRST in this situation is to
   A. promise the employee that you will review all the work assignments in the office to determine whether any changes should be made.
   B. have the employee present his complaint, correcting him whenever he makes what seems to be an erroneous charge against you
   C. postpone discussion of the employee's complaint, explaining to him that the matter can be settled more satisfactory if it is discussed calmly
   D. permit the employee to present his complaint in full, withholding your comments until he has finished making his complaint

6. Assume that you are a supervisor. You find that you are spending too much time on routine tasks and not enough time on supervision of the work of your subordinates.
   It would be ADVISABLE for you to
   A. assign some of the routine tasks to your subordinates
   B. postpone the performance of routine tasks until you have completed your supervisory tasks
   C. delegate the supervisory work to a capable subordinate
   D. eliminate some of the supervisory tasks that you are required to perform

7. Assume that you are a supervisor. You discover that one of your workers has violated an important rule.
   The FIRST course of action for you as the supervisor to take would be to
   A. call a meeting of the entire staff and discuss the matter generally without mentioning any employee by name
   B. arrange to supervise the offending worker's activities more closely
   C. discuss the violation privately with the worker involved
   D. discuss the matter with the worker within hearing of the entire staff so that she will feel too ashamed to commit this violation in the future

8. As a supervisor, you are to prepare a vacation schedule for the bookkeeping office employees.
   The one of the following that is the LEAST important factor for you to consider in setting up this schedule is
   A. seniority   B. vacation preferences of employees
   C. average productivity of the office

9. In assigning a complicated task to a group of subordinates, a certain supervisor does not indicate the specific steps to be followed in performing the assignment, nor does he designate which subordinate is to be responsible for seeing that the task is done on time.

This supervisor's method of assigning the task is MOST likely to result in
- A. confusion among subordinates with consequent delays in work
- B. greater individual effort and self-reliance
- C. assumption of authority by capable subordinates
- D. loss of confidence by subordinates in their ability

10. While you are explaining a new procedure to an employee, she asks you a question about the procedure which you cannot answer.
The MOST appropriate action for you to take is to
    - A. admit your inability to answer the question and promise to obtain the information
    - B. point out the likelihood of a situation arising which would require an answer to the question
    - C. ask the worker to give her reason for asking the question before you give any further reply
    - D. tell her to inform you immediately should a situation arise requiring an answer to her question

KEY (CORRECT ANSWERS)

1.	D	6.	A
2.	B	7.	C
3.	C	8.	C
4.	C	9.	A
5.	D	10.	A

EXAMINATION SECTION
TEST 1

DIRECTIONS: Each question or incomplete statement is followed by several suggested answers or completions. Select the one that BEST answers the question or completes the statement. *PRINT THE LETTER OF THE CORRECT ANSWER IN THE SPACE AT THE RIGHT.*

1. Of the following, the one MOST important quality required of a good supervisor is
    A. ambition   B. leadership   C. friendliness   D. popularity

    1.____

2. It is often said that a supervisor can delegate authority but never responsibility. This means MOST NEARLY that
    A. a supervisor must do his own work if he expects it to be done properly
    B. a supervisor can assign someone else to do his work, but in the last analysis, the supervisor himself must take the blame for any actions followed
    C. authority and responsibility are two separate things that cannot be borne by the same person
    D. it is better for a supervisor never to delegate his authority

    2.____

3. One of your men who is a habitual complainer asks you to grant him a minor privilege.
    Before granting or denying such a request, you should consider
    A. the merits of the case
    B. that it is good for group morale to grant a request of this nature
    C. the man's seniority
    D. that to deny such a request will lower your standing with the men

    3.____

4. A supervisory practice on the part of a foreman which is MOST likely to lead to confusion and inefficiency is for him to
    A. give orders verbally directly to the man assigned to the job
    B. issue orders only in writing
    C. follow up his orders after issuing them
    D. relay his orders to the men through co-workers

    4.____

5. It would be POOR supervision on a foreman's part if he
    A. asked an experienced maintainer for his opinion on the method of doing a special job
    B. make it a policy to avoid criticizing a man in front of his co-workers
    C. consulted his assistant supervisor on unusual problems
    D. allowed a cooling-off period of several days before giving one of his men a deserved reprimand

    5.____

6. Of the following behavior characteristics of a supervisor, the one that is MOST likely to lower the morale of the men he supervises is
   A. diligence
   B. favoritism
   C. punctuality
   D. thoroughness

7. Of the following, the BEST method of getting an employee who is not working up to his capacity to produce more work is to
   A. have another employee criticize his production
   B. privately criticize his production but encourage him to produce more
   C. criticize his production before his associates
   D. criticize his production and threaten to fire him

8. Of the following, the BEST thing for a supervisor to do when a subordinate has done a very good job is to
   A. tell him to take it easy
   B. praise his work
   C. reduce his workload
   D. say nothing because he may become conceited

9. Your orders to your crew are MOST likely to be followed if you
   A. explain the reasons for these orders
   B. warn that all violators will be punished
   C. promise easy assignments to those who follow these orders best
   D. say that they are for the good of the department

10. In order to be a good supervisor, you should
    A. impress upon your men that you demand perfection in their work at all times
    B. avoid being blamed for your crew's mistakes
    C. impress your superior with your ability
    D. see to it that your men get what they are entitled to

11. In giving instructions to a crew, you should
    A. speak in as loud a tone as possible
    B. speak in a coaxing, persuasive manner
    C. speak quietly, clearly, and courteously
    D. always use the word *please* when giving instructions

12. Of the following factors, the one which is LEAST important in evaluating an employee and his work is his
    A. dependability
    B. quantity of work done
    C. quality of work done
    D. education and training

13. When a District Superintendent first assumes his command, it is LEAST important for him at the beginning to observe
    A. how his equipment is designed and its adaptability
    B. how to reorganize the district for greater efficiency
    C. the capabilities of the men in the district
    D. the methods of operation being employed

3 (#1)

14. When making an inspection of one of the buildings under your supervision, the BEST procedure to follow in making a record of the inspection is to
    A. return immediately to the office and write a report from memory
    B. write down all the important facts during or as soon as you complete the inspection
    C. fix in your mind all important facts so that you can repeat them from memory if necessary
    D. fix in your mind all important facts so that you can make out your report at the end of the day

14.____

15. Assume that your superior has directed you to make certain changes in your established procedure. After using this modified procedure on several occasions, you find that the original procedure was distinctly superior and you wish to return to it.
    You should
    A. let your superior find this out for himself
    B. simply change back to the original procedure
    C. compile definite data and information to prove your case to your superior
    D. persuade one of the more experienced workers to take this matter up with your superior

15.____

16. An inspector visited a large building under construction. He inspected the soil lines at 9 A.M., water lines at 10 A.M., fixtures at 11 A.M., and did his office work in the afternoon. He followed the same pattern daily for weeks.
    This procedure was
    A. *good*, because it was methodical and he did not miss anything
    B. *good*, because it gave equal time to all phases of the plumbing
    C. *bad*, because not enough time was devoted to fixtures
    D. *bad*, because the tradesmen knew when the inspection would occur

16.____

17. Assume that one of the foremen in a training course, which you are conducting, proposes a poor solution for a maintenance problem.
    Of the following, the BEST course of action for you to take is to
    A. accept the solution tentatively and correct it during the next class meeting
    B. point out all the defects of this proposed solution and wait until somebody thinks of a better solution
    C. try to get the class to reject this proposed solution and develop a better solution
    D. let the matter pass since somebody will present a better solution as the class work proceeds

17.____

18. As a supervisor, you should be seeking ways to improve the efficiency of shop operations by means such as changing established work procedures.
    The following are offered as possible actions that you should consider in changing established work procedures:
    I. Make changes only when your foremen agree to them
    II. Discuss changes with your supervisor before putting them into practice

18.____

147

III. Standardize any operation which is performed on a continuing basis
IV. Make changes quickly and quietly in order to avoid dissent
V. Secure expert guidance before instituting unfamiliar procedures
Of the following suggested answers, the one that describes the actions to be taken to change established work procedures is
   A. I, IV, V   B. II, III, V   C. III, IV, V   D. All of the above

19. A supervisor determined that a foreman, without informing his superior, delegated responsibility for checking time cards to a member of his gang. The supervisor then called the foreman into his office where he reprimanded the foreman.
This action of the supervisor in reprimanding the foreman was
   A. *proper*, because the checking of time cards is the foreman's responsibility and should not be delegated
   B. *proper*, because the foreman did not ask the supervisor for permission to delegate responsibility
   C. *improper*, because the foreman may no longer take the initiative in solving future problems
   D. *improper*, because the supervisor is interfering in a function which is not his responsibility

19.____

20. A capable supervisor should check all operations under his control.
Of the following, the LEAST important reason for doing this is to make sure that
   A. operations are being performed as scheduled
   B. he personally observes all operations at all times
   C. all the operations are still needed
   D. his manpower is being utilized efficiently

20.____

21. A supervisor makes it a practice to apply fair and firm discipline in all cases of rule infractions, including those of a minor nature.
This practice should PRIMARILY be considered
   A. *bad*, since applying discipline for minor violations is a waste of time
   B. *good*, because not applying discipline for minor infractions can lead to a more serious erosion of discipline
   C. *bad*, because employees do not like to be disciplined for minor violations of the rules
   D. *good*, because violating any rule can cause a dangerous situation to occur

21.____

22. A maintainer would PROPERLY consider it poor supervisory practice for a foreman to consult with him on
   A. which of several repair jobs should be scheduled first
   B. how to cope with personal problems at home
   C. whether the neatness of his headquarters can be improved
   D. how to express a suggestion which the maintainer plans to submit formally

22.____

23. Assume that you have determined that the work of one of your foremen and the men he supervises is consistently behind schedule. When you discuss this situation with the foreman, he tells you that his men are poor workers and then complains that he must spend all of his time checking on their work.
The following actions are offered for your consideration as possible ways of solving the problem of poor performance of the foreman and his men:
   I. Review the work standards with the foreman and determine whether they are realistic.
   II. Tell the foreman that you will recommend him for the foreman's training course for retraining.
   III. Ask the foreman for the names of the maintainers and then replace them as soon as possible.
   IV. Tell the foreman that you expect him to meet a satisfactory level of performance.
   V. Tell the foreman to insist that his men work overtime to catch up to the schedule.
   VI. Tell the foreman to review the type and amount of training he has given the maintainers.
   VII. Tell the foreman that he will be out of a job if he does not produce on schedule.
   VIII. Avoid all criticism of the foreman and his methods.
   Which of the following suggested answers CORRECTLY lists the proper actions to be taken to solve the problem of poor performance of the foreman and his men?
   A. I, II, IV, VI   B. I, III, V, VII   C. II, III, VI, VIII   D. IV, V, VI, VIII

24. When a conference or a group discussion is tending to turn into a *bull session* without constructive purpose, the BEST action to take is to
   A. reprimand the leader of the bull session
   B. redirect the discussion to the business at hand
   C. dismiss the meeting and reschedule it for another day
   D. allow the bull session to continue

25. Assume that you have been assigned responsibility for a program in which a high production rate is mandatory. From past experience, you know that your foremen do not perform equally well in the various types of jobs given to them. Which of the following methods should you use in selecting foremen for the specific types of work involved in the program?
   A. Leave the method of selecting foremen to your supervisor
   B. Assign each foreman to the work he does best
   C. Allow each foreman to choose his own job
   D. Assign each foreman to a job which will permit him to improve his own abilities

KEY (CORRECT ANSWERS)

1.	B	11.	C
2.	B	12.	D
3.	A	13.	B
4.	D	14.	B
5.	D	15.	C
6.	B	16.	D
7.	B	17.	C
8.	B	18.	B
9.	A	19.	A
10.	D	20.	B

21.	B
22.	A
23.	A
24.	B
25.	B

TEST 2

DIRECTIONS: Each question or incomplete statement is followed by several suggested answers or completions. Select the one that BEST answers the question or completes the statement. *PRINT THE LETTER OF THE CORRECT ANSWER IN THE SPACE AT THE RIGHT.*

1. A foreman who is familiar with modern management principles should know that the one of the following requirements of an administrator which is LEAST important is his ability to
    A. coordinate work
    B. plan, organize, and direct the work under his control
    C. cooperate with others
    D. perform the duties of the employees under his jurisdiction

    1._____

2. When subordinates request his advice in solving problems encountered in their work, a certain chief occasionally answers the request by first asking the subordinate what he thinks should be done.
    This action by the chief is, on the whole,
    A. *desirable*, because it stimulates subordinates to give more thought to the solution of problems encountered
    B. *undesirable*, because it discourages subordinates from asking questions
    C. *desirable*, because it discourages subordinates from asking questions
    D. *undesirable*, because it undermines the confidence of subordinates in the ability of their supervisor

    2._____

3. Of the following factors that may be considered by a unit head in dealing with the tardy subordinate, the one which should be given LEAST consideration is the
    A. frequency with which the employee is tardy
    B. effect of the employee's tardiness upon the work of other employees
    C. willingness of the employee to work overtime when necessary
    D. cause of the employee's tardiness

    3._____

4. The MOST important requirement of a good inspectional report is that it should be
    A. properly addressed   B. lengthy
    C. clear and brief   D. spelled correctly

    4._____

5. Building superintendents frequently inquire about departmental inspectional procedures.
    Of the following, it is BEST to
    A. advise them to write to the department for an official reply
    B. refuse as the inspectional procedure is a restricted matter
    C. briefly explain the procedure to them
    D. avoid the inquiry by changing the subject

    5._____

6. Reprimanding a crew member before other workers is a
   A. *good* practice; the reprimand serves as a warning to the other workers
   B. *bad* practice; people usually resent criticism made in public
   C. *good* practice; the other workers will realize that the supervisor is fair
   D. *bad* practice; the other workers will take sides in the dispute

7. Of the following actions, the one which is LEAST likely to promote good work is for the group leader to
   A. praise workers for doing a good job
   B. call attention to the opportunities for promotion for better workers
   C. threaten to recommend discharge of workers who are below standard
   D. put into practice any good suggestion made by crew members

8. A supervisor notices that a member of his crew has skipped a routine step in his job.
   Of the following, the BEST action for the supervisor to take is to
   A. promptly question the worker about the incident
   B. immediately assign another man to complete the job
   C. bring up the incident the next time the worker asks for a favor
   D. say nothing about the incident but watch the worker carefully in the future

9. Assume you have been told to show a new worker how to operate a piece of equipment.
   Your FIRST step should be to
   A. ask the worker if he has any questions about the equipment
   B. permit the worker to operate the equipment himself while you carefully watch to prevent damage
   C. demonstrate the operation of the equipment for the worker
   D. have the worker read an instruction booklet on the maintenance of the equipment

10. Whenever a new man was assigned to his crew, the supervisor would introduce him to all other crew members, take him on a tour of the plant, tell him about bus schedules and places to eat.
    This practice is
    A. *good*; the new man is made to feel welcome
    B. *bad*; supervisors should not interfere in personal matters
    C. *good*; the new man knows that he can bring his personal problems to the supervisor
    D. *bad*; work time should not be spent on personal matters

11. The MOST important factor in successful leadership is the ability to
    A. obtain instant obedience to all orders
    B. establish friendly personal relations with crew members
    C. avoid disciplining crew members
    D. make crew members want to do what should be done

3 (#2)

12. Explaining the reasons for departmental procedure to workers tends to   12.____
    A. waste time which should be used for productive purposes
    B. increase their interest in their work
    C. make them more critical of departmental procedures
    D. confuse them

13. If you want a job done well do it yourself.   13.____
    For a supervisor to follow this advice would be
    A. *good*; a supervisor is responsible for the work of his crew
    B. *bad*; a supervisor should train his men, not do their work
    C. *good*; a supervisor should be skilled in all jobs assigned to his crew
    D. *bad*; a supervisor loses respect when he works with his hands

14. When a supervisor discovers a mistake in one of the jobs for which his crew   14.____
    is responsible, it is MOST important for him to find out
    A. whether anybody else knows about the mistake
    B. who was to blame for the mistake
    C. how to prevent similar mistakes in the future
    D. whether similar mistakes occurred in the past

15. A supervisor who has to explain a new procedure to his crew should realize   15.____
    that questions from the crew USUALLY show that they
    A. are opposed to the new practice
    B. are completely confused by the explanation
    C. need more training in the new procedure
    D. are interested in the explanation

16. A good way for a supervisor to retain the confidence of his or her employees   16.____
    is to
    A. say as little as possible
    B. check work frequently
    C. make no promises unless they will be fulfilled
    D. never hesitate in giving an answer to any question

17. Good supervision is ESSENTIALLY a matter of   17.____
    A. patience in supervising workers   B. care in selecting workers
    C. skill in human relations   D. fairness in disciplining workers

18. It is MOST important for an employee who has been assigned a monotonous   18.____
    task to
    A. perform this task before doing other work
    B. ask another employee to help
    C. perform this task only after all other work has been completed
    D. take measures to prevent mistakes in performing the task

4 (#2)

19. One of your employees has violated a minor agency regulation.
The FIRST thing you should do is
   A. warn the employee that you will have to take disciplinary action if it should happen again
   B. ask the employee to explain his or her actions
   C. inform your supervisor and wait for advice
   D. write a memo describing the incident and place it in the employee's personnel file

19.____

20. One of your employees tells you that he feels you give him much more work than the other employees, and he is having trouble meeting your deadlines.
You should
   A. ask if he has been under a lot of non-work related stress lately
   B. review his recent assignments to determine if he is correct
   C. explain that this is a busy time, but you are dividing the work equally
   D. tell him that he is the most competent employee and that is why he receives more work

20.____

21. A supervisor assigns one of his crew to complete a portion of a job. A short time later, the supervisor notices that the portion has not been completed.
Of the following, the BEST way for the supervisor to handle this is to
   A. ask the crew member why he has not completed the assignment
   B. reprimand the crew member for not obeying orders
   C. assign another crew member to complete the assignment
   D. complete the assignment himself

21.____

22. Supposes that a member of your crew complains that you are *playing favorites* in assigning work.
Of the following, the BEST method of handling the complaint is to
   A. deny it and refuse to discuss the matter with the worker
   B. take the opportunity to tell the worker what is wrong with his work
   C. ask the worker for examples to prove his point and try to clear up any misunderstanding
   D. promise to be more careful in making assignments in the future

22.____

23. A member of your crew comes to you with a complaint. After discussing the matter with him, it is clear that you have convinced him that his complaint was not justified.
At this point, you should
   A. permit him to drop the matter
   B. make him admit his error
   C. pretend to see some justification in his complaint
   D. warn him against making unjustified complaints

23.____

24. Suppose that a supervisor has in his crew an older man who works rather slowly. In other respects, this man is a good worker; he is seldom absent, works carefully, never loafs, and is cooperative.

24.____

The BEST way for the supervisor to handle this worker is to
- A. try to get him to work faster and less carefully
- B. give him the most disagreeable job
- C. request that he be given special training
- D. permit him to work at his own speed

25. Suppose that a member of your crew comes to you with a suggestion he thinks will save time in doing a job. You realize immediately that it won't work. Under these circumstances, your BEST action would be to
    - A. thank the worker for the suggestion and forget about it
    - B. explain to the worker why you think it won't work
    - C. tell the worker to put the suggestion in writing
    - D. ask the other members of your crew to criticize the suggestion

25.____

KEY (CORRECT ANSWERS)

1.	D		11.	D
2.	A		12.	B
3.	C		13.	B
4.	C		14.	C
5.	C		15.	D
6.	B		16.	C
7.	C		17.	C
8.	A		18.	D
9.	C		19.	B
10.	A		20.	B

21. A
22. C
23. A
24. D
25. B

SUPERVISION STUDY GUIDE

Social science has developed information about groups and leadership in general and supervisor-employee relationships in particular. Since organizational effectiveness is closely linked to the ability of supervisors to direct the activities of employees, these findings are important to executives everywhere.

IS A SUPERVISOR A LEADER?

First-line supervisors are found in all large business and government organizations. They are the men at the base of an organizational hierarchy. Decisions made by the head of the organization reach them through a network of intermediate positions. They are frequently referred to as part of the management team, but their duties seldom seem to support this description.

A supervisor of clerks, tax collectors, meat inspectors, or securities analysts is not charged with budget preparation. He cannot hire or fire the employees in his own unit on his say-so. He does not administer programs which require great planning, coordinating, or decision making.

Then what is he? He is the man who is directly in charge of a group of employees doing productive work for a business or government agency. If the work requires the use of machines, the men he supervises operate them. If the work requires the writing of reports, the men he supervises write them. He is expected to maintain a productive flow of work without creating problems which higher levels of management must solve. But is he a leader?

To carry out a specific part of an agency's mission, management creates a unit, staffs it with a group of employees and designates a supervisor to take charge of them. Management directs what this unit shall do, from time to time changes directions, and often indicates what the group should not do. Management presumably creates status for the supervisor by giving him more pay, a title, and special privileges.

Management asks a supervisor to get his workers to attain organizational goals, including the desired quantity and quality of production. Supposedly, he has authority to enable him to achieve this objective. Management at least assumes that by establishing the status of the supervisor's position, it has created sufficient authority to enable him to achieve these goals—not his goals, nor necessarily the group's, but management's goals.

In addition, supervision includes writing reports, keeping records of membership in a higher-level administrative group, industrial engineering, safety engineering, editorial duties, housekeeping duties, etc. The supervisor as a member of an organizational network, must be responsible to the changing demands of the management above him. At the same time, he must be responsive to the demands of the work group of which he is a member. He is placed in the difficult position of communicating and implementing new decisions, changed programs and revised production quotas for his work group, although he may have had little part in developing them.

It follows, then, that supervision has a special characteristic: achievement of goals, previously set by management, through the efforts of others. It is in this feature of the supervisor's job that we find the role of a leader in the sense of the following definition: *A leader is that person who most effectively influences group activities toward goal setting and goal achievements.*

This definition is broad. It covers both leaders in groups that come together voluntarily and in those brought together through a work assignment in a factory, store, or government agency. In the natural group, the authority necessary to attain goals is determined by the group membership and is granted by them. In the working group, it is apparent that the establishment of a supervisory position creates a predisposition on the part of employees to accept the authority of the occupant of that position. We cannot, however, assume that mere occupation confers authority sufficient to assure the accomplishment of an organization's goals.

Supervision is different, then, from leadership. The supervisor is expected to fulfill the role of leader but without obtaining a grant of authority from the group he supervises. The supervisor is expected to influence the group in the achieving of goals but is often handicapped by having little influence on the organizational process by which goals are set. The supervisor, because he works in an organizational setting, has the burdens of additional organizational duties and restrictions and requirements arising out of the fact that his position is subordinate to a hierarchy of higher-level supervisors. These differences between leadership and supervision are reflected in our definition: *Supervision is basically a leadership role, in a formal organization, which has as its objective the effective influencing of other employees.*

Even though these differences between supervision and leadership exist, a significant finding of experimenters in this field is that supervisors must be leaders to be successful.

The problem is: How can a supervisor exercise leadership in an organizational setting? We might say that the supervisor is expected to be a natural leader in a situation which does not come about naturally. His situation becomes really difficult in an organization which is more eager to make its supervisors into followers rather than leaders.

LEADERSHIP: NATURAL AND ORGANIZATIONAL

Leadership, in its usual sense of *natural* leadership, and supervision are not the same. In some cases, leadership embraces broader powers and functions than supervision; in other cases, supervision embraces more than leadership. This is true both because of the organization and technical aspects of the supervisor's job and because of the relatively freer setting and inherent authority of the natural leader.

The natural leader usually has much more authority and influence than the supervisor. Group members not only follow his command but prefer it that way. The employee, however, can appeal the supervisor's commands to his union or to the supervisor's superior or to the personnel office. These intercessors represent restrictions on the supervisor's power to lead.

The natural leader can gain greater membership involvement in the group's objectives, and he can change the objectives of the group. The supervisor can attempt to gain employee support only for management's objectives; he cannot set other objectives. In these instances leadership is broader than supervision.

The natural leader must depend upon whatever skills are available when seeking to attain objectives. The supervisor is trained in the administrative skills necessary to achieve management's goals. If he does not possess the requisite skills, however, he can call upon management's technicians.

A natural leader can maintain his leadership, in certain groups, merely by satisfying members' need for group affiliation. The supervisor must maintain his leadership by directing and organizing his group to achieve specific organizational goals set for him and his group by management. He must have a technical competence and a kind of coordinating ability which is not needed by many natural leaders.

A natural leader is responsible only to his group which grants him authority. The supervisor is responsible to management, which employs him, and also to the work group of which he is a member. The supervisor has the exceedingly difficult job of reconciling the demands of two groups frequently in conflict. He is often placed in the untenable position of trying to play two antagonistic roles. In the above instance, supervision is broader than leadership.

ORGANIZATIONAL INFLUENCES ON LEADERSHIP

The supervisor is both a product and a prisoner of the organization wherein we find him. The organization which creates the supervisor's position also obstructs, restricts, and channelizes the exercise of his duties. These influences extend beyond prescribed functional relationships to specific supervisory behavior. For example, even in a face-to-face situation involving one of his subordinates, the supervisor's actions are controlled to a great extent by his organization. His behavior must conform to the organization policy on human relations, rules which dictate personnel procedures, specific prohibitions governing conduct, the attitudes of his own superior, etc. He is not a free agent operating within the limits of his work group. His freedom of action is much more circumscribed than is generally admitted. The organizational influences which limit his leadership actions can be classified as structure, prescriptions, and proscriptions.

The organizational structure places each supervisor's position in context with other designated positions. It determines the relationships between his position and specific positions which impinge on his. The structure of the organization designates a certain position to which he looks for orders and information about his work. It gives a particular status to his position within a pattern of statuses from which he perceives that (1) certain positions are on a par, organizationally, with his, (2) other positions are subordinate, and (3) still others are superior.

The organizational structure determines those positions to which he should look for advice and assistance, and those positions to which he should give advice and assistance.

For instance, the organizational structure has predetermined that the supervisor of a clerical processing unit shall report to a supervisory position in a higher echelon. He shall have certain relationships with the supervisors of the work units which transmit work to and receive work from his unit. He shall discuss changes and clarification of procedures with certain staff units, such as organization and methods, cost accounting, and personnel. He shall consult supervisors of units which provide or receive special work assignments.

The organizational structure, however, establishes patterns other than those of the relationships of positions. These are the patterns of responsibility, authority, and expectations.

The supervisor is responsible for certain activities or results; he is presumably invested with the authority to achieve these. His set of authority and responsibility is interwoven with other sets to the end that all goals and functions of the organization are parceled out in small, manageable lots. This, of course, establishes a series of expectations: a single supervisor can perform his particular set of duties only upon the assumption that preceding or contiguous sets of duties have been, or are being carried out. At the same time, he is aware of the expectations of others that he will fulfill his functional role.

The structure of an organization establishes relationships between specified positions and specific expectations for these positions. The fact that these relationships and expectations are established is one thing; whether or not they are met is another.

PRESCRIPTIONS AND PROSCRIPTIONS

But let us return to the organizational influences which act to restrict the supervisor's exercise of leadership. These are the prescriptions and proscriptions generally in effect in all organizations, and those peculiar to a single organization. In brief these are the *thou shalt's* and the *thou shalt not's*.

Organizations not only prescribe certain duties for individual supervisory positions, they also prescribe specific methods and means of carrying out these duties and maintaining management-employee relations. These include rules, regulations, policy, and tradition. It does no good for the supervisor to say, *This seems to be the best way to handle such-and-such,* if the organization has established a routine for dealing with problems. For good or bad, there are rules that state that firings shall be executed in such a manner, accompanied by a certain notification; that training shall be conducted, and in this manner. Proscriptions are merely negative prescriptions; you may not discriminate against any employee because of politics or race; you shall not suspend any employee without following certain procedures and obtaining certain approvals.

Most of these prohibitions and rules apply to the area of interpersonal relations, precisely the area which is now arousing most interest on the part of administrators and managers. We have become concerned about the contrast between formally prescribed relationships and interpersonal relationships, and this brings us to the often discussed informal organization.

FORMAL AND INFORMAL ORGANIZATIONS

As we well know, the functions and activities of any organization are broken down into individual units of work called positions. Administrators must establish a pattern which will link these positions to each other and relate them to a system of authority and responsibility. Man-to-man are spelled out as plainly as possible for all to understand. Managers, then, build an official structure which we call the formal organization.

In these same organizations, employees react individually and in groups to institutionally determined roles. John, a worker, rides in the same carpool as Joe, a foreman. An unplanned communication develops. Harry, a machinist knows more about high-speed machining than his foreman or anyone else in his shop. An unofficial tool boss comes into being. Mary, who fought with Jane, is promoted over her. Jane now gives Mary's directions. A planned relationship fails to develop. The employees have built a structure which we call the informal organization.

> *Formal organization is a system of management-prescribed relations between positions in an organization.*
>
> *Informal organization is a network of unofficial relations between people in an organization.*

These definitions might lead us to the absurd conclusion that positions carry out formal activities and that employe4es spend their time in unofficial activities. We must recognize that organizational activities are in all cases carried out by people. The formal structure provides a needed framework within which interpersonal relations occur. What we call informal organization is the complex of normal, natural relations among employees. These personal relationships may be negative or positive. That is, they may impede or aid the achievement of organizational goals. For example, friendship between two supervisors greatly increases the probability of good cooperation and coordination between their sections. On the other hand, *buck passing* nullifies the formal structure by failure to meet a prescribed and expected responsibility.

It is improbable that an ideal organization exists where all activities are carried out in strict conformity to a formally prescribed pattern of functional roles. Informal organization arises because of the incompleteness and ambiguities in the network of formally prescribed relationships, or in response to the needs or inadequacies of supervisors or managers who hold prescribed functional roles in an organization. Many of these relationships are not prescribed by the organizational pattern; many cannot be prescribed; many should not be prescribed.

Management faces the problem of keeping the informal organization in harmony with the mission of the agency. One way to do this is to make sure that all employees have a clear understanding of and are sympathetic with that mission. The issuance of organizational charts, procedural manuals, and functional descriptions of the work to be done by divisions and sections helps communicate management's plans and goals. Issuances alone, of course, cannot do the whole job. They should be accompanied by oral discussion and explanation. Management must ensure that there is mutual understanding and acceptance of charts and procedures. More important is that management acquaint itself with the attitudes, activities, and peculiar brands of logic which govern the informal organization. Only through this type of knowledge can they and supervisors keep informal goals consistent with the agency mission.

SUPERVISION STATUS AND FUNCTIONAL ROLE

A well-established supervisor is respected by the employees who work with him. They defer to his wishes. It is clear that a superior-subordinate relationship has been established. That is, status of the supervisor has been established in relation to other employees of the same work group. This same supervisor gains the respect of employees when he behaves in as certain manner. He will be expected, generally, to follow the customs of the group in such matters as dress, recreation, and manner of speaking. The group has a set of expectations as to his behavior. His position is a functional role which carries with it a collection of rights and obligations.

The position of supervisor usually has a status distinct from the individual who occupies it: it is much like a position description which exists whether or not there is an incumbent. The status of a supervisory position is valued higher than that of an employee position both because of the functional role of leadership which is assigned to it and because of the status symbols of titles, rights, and privileges which go with it.

Social ranking, or status, is not simple because it involves both the position and the man. An individual may be ranked higher than others because of his education, social background, perceived leadership ability, or conformity to group customs and ideals. If such a man is ranked higher by the members of a work group than their supervisor, the supervisor's effectiveness may be seriously undermined.

If the organization does not build and reinforce a supervisor's status, his position can be undermined in a different way. This will happen when managers go around rather than through the supervisor or designate him as a straw boss, acting boss, or otherwise not a real boss.

Let us clarify this last point. A role, and corresponding status, establishes a set of expectations. Employees expect their supervisor to do certain things and to act in certain ways. They are prepared to respond to that expected behavior. When the supervisor's behavior does not conform to their expectations, they are surprised, confused, and ill-at-ease. It becomes necessary for them to resolve their confusion, if they can. They might do this by turning to one of their own members for leadership. If the confusion continues, or their attempted solutions are not satisfactory, they will probably become a poorly motivated, non-cohesive group which cannot function very well.

COMMUNICATION AND THE SUPERVISOR

In a recent survey, railroad workers reported that they rarely look to their supervisor for information about the company. This is startling, at least to us, because we ordinarily think of the supervisor as the link between management and worker. We expect the supervisor to be the prime source of information about the company. Actually, the railroad workers listed the supervisor next to last in the o5rder of their sources of information. Most surprising of all, the supervisors, themselves, stated that rumor and unofficial contacts were their principal sources of information. Here we see one of the reasons why supervisors may not be as effective as management desires.

The supervisor is not only being bypassed by his work group, he is being ignored, and his position weakened, by the very organization which is holding him responsible for the activities of his workers. If he is management's representative to the employee, then management has an obligation to keep him informed of its activities. This is necessary if he is to carry out his functions efficiently and maintain his leadership in the work group. The supervisor is expected to be a source of information; when he is not, his status is not clear, and employees are dissatisfied because he has not lived up to expectations.

By providing information to the supervisor to pass along to employees, we can strengthen his position as leader of the group, and increase satisfaction and cohesion within the group. Because he has more information than the other members, receives information sooner, and passes it along at the proper times, members turn to him as a source and also provide him with information in the hope of receiving some in return. From this, we can see an increase in group cohesiveness because:

- Employees are bound closer to their supervisor because he is *in the know*.
- There is less need to go outside the group for answers
- Employees will more quickly turn to the supervisor for enlightenment

The fact that he has the answers will also enhance the supervisor's standing in the eyes of his men. This increased status will serve to bolster his authority and control of the group and will probably result in improved morale and productivity.

The foregoing, of course, does not mean that all management information should be given out. There are obviously certain policy determinations and discussions which need not or cannot be transmitted to all supervisors. However, the supervisor must be kept as fully informed as possible so that he can answer questions when asked and can allay needless fears and anxieties. Further, the supervisor has the responsibility of encouraging employee questions and submissions of information. He must be able to present information to employees so that it is clearly understood and accepted. His attitude and manner should make it clear that he believes in what he is saying, that the information is necessary or desirable to the group, and that he is prepared to act on the basis of the information.

SUPERVISION AND JOB PERFORMANCE

The productivity of work groups is a product; employees' efforts are multiplied by the supervision they receive. Many investigators have analyzed this relationship and have discovered elements of supervision which differentiate high and low production groups. These researchers have identified certain types of supervisory practices which they classify as *employee-centered* and other types which they classify as *production centered*.

The difference between these two kinds of supervision lies not in specific practices but in the approach or orientation to supervision. The employee-centered supervisor directs most of his efforts toward increasing employee motivation. He is concerned more with realizing the potential energy of persons than with administrative and technological methods of increasing efficiency and productivity. He is the man who finds ways of causing employees to want to work harder with the same tools. These supervisors emphasize the personal relations between their employees and themselves.

Now, obviously, these pictures are overdrawn. No one supervisor has all the virtues of the ideal type of employee-centered supervisor. And, fortunately, no one supervisor has all the bad traits found in many production-centered supervisors. We should remember that the various practices that researchers have fond which distinguish these two kinds of supervision represent the many practices and methods of supervisors of all gradations between these extremes. We should be careful, too, of the implications of the labels attached to the two types. For instance, being production-centered is not necessarily bad, since the principal responsibility of any supervisor is maintaining the production level that is expected of his work group. Being employee-centered may not necessarily be good, if the only result is a happy, chuckling crew of loafers. To return to the researchers' findings, employee-centered supervisors:

- Recommend promotions, transfers, pay increases
- Inform men about what is happening in the company
- Keep men posted on how well they are doing
- Hear complaints and grievances sympathetically
- Speak up for subordinates

Production-centered supervisors, on the other hand, don't do those things. They check on employees more frequently, give more detailed and frequent instructions, don't give reasons for changes, and are more punitive when mistakes are made. Employee-centered supervisors were reported to contribute to high morale and high production, whereas production-centered supervision was associated with lower morale and less production.

More recent findings, however, show that the relationship between supervision and productivity is not this simple. Investigators now report that high production is more frequently associated with supervisory practices which combine employee-centered behavior with concern for production. (This concern is not the same, however, as anxiety about production, which is the hallmark of our production-centered supervisor.) Let us examine these apparently contradictory findings and the premises from which they are derived.

SUPERVISION AND MORALE

Why do supervisory activities cause high or low production? As the name implies, the activities of the employee-centered supervisor tend to relate him more closely and satisfactorily to his workers. The production-centered supervisor's practices tend to separate him from his group and to foster antagonism. An analysis of this difference may answer our question.

Earlier, we pointed out that the supervisor is a type of leader and that leadership is intimately related to the group in which it occurs We discover, now, that an employee-centered supervisor's primary activities are concerned with both his leadership and his group membership. Such a supervisor is a member of a group and occupies a leadership role in that group.

These facts are sometimes obscured when we speak of the supervisor as management's representative, or as the organizational link between management and the employee, or as the end of the chain of command. If we really want to understand what it is we expect of the supervisor, we must remember that he is the designated leader of a group of employees to whom he is bound by interaction and interdependence.

Most of his actions are aimed, consciously or unconsciously, at strengthening membership ties in the group. This includes both making members more conscious that he is a member of their group) and causing members to identify themselves more closely with the group. These ends are accomplished by:

- making the group more attractive to the worker: they find satisfaction of their needs for recognition, friendship, enjoyable work, etc.;
- maintaining open communication: employees can express their views and obtain information about the organization
- giving assistance: members can seek advice on personal problems as well as their work; and
- acting as a buffer between the group and management: he speaks up for his men and explains the reasons for management's decisions.

Such actions both strengthen group cohesiveness and solidarity and affirm the supervisor's leadership position in the group.

DEFINING MORALE

This brings us back to a point mentioned earlier. We had said that employee-centered supervisors contribute to high morale as well as to high production. But how can we explain units which have low morale and high productivity, or vice versa? Usually production and morale are considered separately, partly because they are measured against different criteria and partly because, in some instances, they seem to be independent of each other.

Some of this difficulty may stem from confusion over definitions of morale. Morale has been defined as, or measured by, absences from work, satisfaction with job or company, dissension among members of work groups, productivity, apathy or lack of interest, readiness to help others, and a general aura of happiness as rated by observers. Some of these criteria of morale are not subject to the influence of the supervisor, and some of them are not clearly related to productivity. Definitions like these invite findings of low morale coupled with high production.

Both productivity and morale can be influenced by environmental factors not under the control of group members or supervisors. Such things as plant layout, organizational structure and goals, lighting, ventilation, communications, and management planning may have an adverse or desirable effect.

We might resolve the dilemma by defining morale on the basis of our understanding of the supervisor as leader of a group; morale is the degree of satisfaction of group members with their leadership. In this light, the supervisor's employee-centered activities bear a clear relation to morale. His efforts to increase employee identification with the group and to strengthen his leadership lead to greater satisfaction with that leadership. By increasing group cohesiveness and by demonstrating that his influence and power can aid the group, he is able to enhance his leadership status and afford satisfaction to the group.

SUPERVISION, PRODUCTION, AND MORALE

There are factors within the organization itself which determine whether increased production is possible:

- Are production goals expressed in terms understandable to employees and are they realistic?
- Do supervisors responsible for production respect the agency mission and production goals?
- If employees do not know how to do the job well, does management provide a trainer—often the supervisor—who can teach efficient work methods?

There are other factors within the work group which determine whether increased production will be attained:

- Is leadership present which can bring about the desired level of production?
- Are production goals accepted by employees as reasonable and attainable?
- If group effort is involved, are members able to coordinate their efforts?

Research findings confirm the view that an employee-centered supervisor can achieve higher morale than a production-centered supervisor. Managers may well ask what is the relationship between this and production.

Supervision is production-oriented to the extent that it focuses attention on achieving organizational goals, and plans and devises methods for attaining them; it is employee-centered to the extent that it focuses attention on employee attitudes toward those goals, and plans and works toward maintenance of employee satisfaction.

High productivity and low morale result when a supervisor plans and organizes work efficiently but cannot achieve high membership satisfaction. Low production and high morale result when a supervisor, though keeping members satisfied with his leadership, either has not gained acceptance of organizational goals or does not have the technical competence to achieve them.

The relationship between supervision, morale, and productivity is an interdependent one, with the supervisor playing an integral role due to his ability to influence productivity and morale independently of each other.

A supervisor who can plan his work well has good technical knowledge, and who can install better production methods can raise production without necessarily increasing group satisfaction. On the other hand, a supervisor who can motivate his employees and keep them satisfied with his leadership can gain high production in spite of technical difficulties and environmental obstacles.

CLIMATE AND SUPERVISION

Climate, the intangible environment of an organization made up of attitudes, beliefs, and traditions, plays a large part in morale, productivity, and supervision. Usually when we speak of climate and its relationship to morale and productivity, we talk about the merits of *democratic* versus *authoritarian* climate. Employees seem to produce more and have higher morale in a democratic climate, whereas in an authoritarian climate, the reverse seems to be true or so the researchers tell us. We would do well to determine what these terms mean to supervision.

Perhaps most of our difficulty in understanding and applying these concepts comes from our emotional reactions to the words themselves. For example, authoritarian climate is usually painted as the very blackest kind of dictatorship. This is not surprising, because we are usually expected to believe that it is invariably bad. Conversely, democratic climate is drawn to make the driven snow look impure by comparison.

Now these descriptions are most probably true when we talk about our political processes, or town meetings, or freedom of speech. However, the same labels have been used by social scientists in other contexts and have also been applied to government and business organizations, without it, it seems, any recognition that the meanings and their social values may have changed somewhat

For example, these labels were used in experiments conducted in an informal classroom setting using 11-year-old boys as subjects. The descriptive labels applied to the climate of the setting as well as the type of leadership practiced. When these labels were transferred to a management setting, it seems that many presumed that they principally meant the king of leadership rather than climate. We can see that there is a great difference between the experimental and management settings and that leadership practices for one might be inappropriate for the other.

It is doubtful that formal work organizations can be anything but authoritarian, in that goals are set by management and a hierarchy exists through which decisions and orders from the top are transmitted downward. Organizations are authoritarian by structure and need; direction and control are placed in the hands of a few in order to gain fast and efficient decision making. Now this does not mean to describe a dictatorship. It is merely the recognition of the fact that direction of organizational affairs comes from above. It should be noted that leadership in some natural groups is, in this sense, authoritarian.

Granting that formal organizations have this kind of authoritarian leadership, can there be a democratic climate? Certainly there can be, but we would want to define and delimit this term. A more realistic meaning of democratic climate in organizations is the use of permissive and participatory methods in management-employee relations. That is, a mutual exchange of information and explanation with the granting of individual freedom within certain restricted and defined limits. However, it is not our purpose to debate the merits of authoritarianism versus democracy. We recognize that within the small work group there is a need for freedom from constraint and an increase in participation in order to achieve organizational goals within the framework of the organizational movement.

Another aspect of climate is best expressed by this familiar, and true, saying: actions speak louder than words. Of particular concern to us is this effect of management climate on the behavior of supervisors, particularly in employee-centered activities.

There have been reports of disappointment with efforts to make supervisors ore employee-centered. Managers state that, since research has shown ways of improving human relations, supervisors should begin to practice these methods. Usually a training course in human relations is established; and supervisors are given this training. Managers then sit back and wait for the expected improvements, only to find that there are none.

If we wish to produce changes in the supervisor's behavior, the climate must be made appropriate and rewarding to the changed behavior. This means that top-level attitudes and behavior cannot deny or contradict the change we are attempting to effect. Basic changes in organizational behavior cannot be made with any permanence, unless we provide an environment that is receptive to the changes and rewards those persons who do change.

IMPROVING SUPERVISION

Anyone who has read this far might expect to find *A Dozen Rules for Dealing With Employees* or *29 Steps to Supervisory Success*. We will not provide such a list.

Simple rules suffer from their simplicity. They ignore the complexities of human behavior. Reliance upon rules may cause supervisors to concentrate on superficial aspects of their relations with employees. It may preclude genuine understanding.

The supervisor who relies on a list of rules tends to think of people in mechanistic terms. In a certain situation, he uses *Rule No. 3*. Employees are not treated as thinking and feeling persons, but rather as figures in a formula: Rule 3 applied to employee X = Production.

Employees usually recognize mechanical manipulation and become dissatisfied and resentful. They lose faith in, and respect for, their supervisor, and this may be reflected in lower morale and productivity.

We do not mean that supervisors must become social science experts if they wish to improve. Reports of current research indicate that there are two major parts of their job which can be strengthened through self-improvement: (1) Work planning, including technical skills, and (2) motivation of employees.

The most effective supervisors combine excellence in the administrative and technical aspects of their work with friendly and considerate personal relations with their employees.

CRITICAL PERSONAL RELATIONS

Later in this chapter we shall talk about administrative aspects of supervision, but first let us comment on *friendly and considerate personal relations*. We have discussed this subject throughout the preceding chapters, but we want to review some of the critical supervisory influences on personal relations.

Closeness of Supervision: The closeness of supervision has an important effect on productivity and morale. Mann and Dent found that supervisors of low-producing units supervise very closely, while high-producing supervisors exercise only general supervision. It was found that the low-producing supervisors:

- check on employees more frequently
- give more detailed and frequent instructions
- limit employee's freedom to do job in own way

Workers who felt less closely supervised reported that they were better satisfied with their jobs and the company. We should note that the manner or attitude of the supervisor has an important bearing on whether employees perceive supervision as being close or general.

These findings are another way of saying that supervision does not mean standing over the employee and telling him what to do and when and how to do it. The more effective supervisor tells his employees what is required, giving general instructions.

COMMUNICATION

Supervisors of high-production units consider communication as one of the most important aspects of their job. Effective communication is used by these supervisors to achieve better interpersonal relations and improved employee motivation. Low-production supervisors do not rate communications as highly important.

High-producing supervisors find that an important aid to more effective communication is listening. They are ready to listen to both personal problems or interests and questions about the work. This does not mean that they are *nosey* or meddle in their employees' personal lives, but rather that they show a willingness to listen, and do listen, if their employees wish to discuss problems.

These supervisors inform employees about forthcoming changes in work; they discuss agency policy with employees; and they make sure that each employee knows how well he is doing. What these supervisors do is use two-way communication effectively. Unless the supervisor freely imparts information, he will not receive information in return.

Attitudes and perception are frequently affected by communication or the lack of it. Research surveys reveal that many supervisors are not aware of their employees' attitudes, nor do they know what personal reactions their supervision arouses. Through frank discussion with employees, they have been surprised to discover employee beliefs about which they were ignorant. Discussion sometimes reveals that the supervisor and his employees have totally different impressions about the same event. The supervisor should be constantly on the alert for misconceptions about his words and deeds. He must remember that, although his actions are perfectly clear to himself, they may be, and frequently are, viewed differently by employees.

Failure to communicate information results in misconceptions and false assumptions. What you say and how you say it will strongly affect your employees' attitudes and perceptions. By giving them available information, you can prevent misconceptions; by discussion, you may be able to change attitudes; by questioning, you can discover what the perceptions and assumptions really are. And it need hardly be added that actions should conform very closely to words.

If we were to attempt to reduce the above discussion on communication to rules, we would have a long list which would be based on one cardinal principle: Don't make assumptions!

- Don't assume that your employees know; tell them.
- Don't assume that you know how they feel; find out.
- Don't assume that they understand; clarify.

20 SUPERVISORY HINTS

1. Avoid inconsistency.
2. Always give employees a chance to explain their action before taking disciplinary action. Don't allow too much time for a "cooling off" period before disciplining an employee.
3. Be specific in your criticisms.
4. Delegate responsibility wisely.
5. Do not argue or lose your temper, and avoid being impatient.
6. Promote mutual respect and be fair, impartial, and open-minded.
7. Keep in mind that asking for employees' advice and input can be helpful in decision making.
8. If you make promises, keep them.
9. Always keep the feelings, abilities, dignity and motives of your staff in mind.
10. Remain loyal to your employees' interests.
11. Never criticize employees in front of others, or treat employees like children.
12. Admit mistakes. Don't place blame on your employees, or make excuses.
13. Be reasonable in your expectations, give complete instructions, and establish well-planned goals.
14. Be knowledgeable about office details and procedures, but avoid becoming bogged down in details.
15. Avoid supervising too closely or too loosely. Employees should also view you as an approachable supervisor.
16. Remember that employees' personal problems may affect job performance, but become involved only when appropriate.
17. Work to develop workers, and to instill a feeling of cooperation while working toward mutual goals.
18. Do not overpraise or underpraise, be properly appreciative.
19. Never ask an employee to discipline someone for you.
20. A complaint, even if unjustified, should be taken seriously.

NOTES